THE CIVILIZATION OF THE AMERICAN INDIAN SERIES

Chief Bowles and the Texas Cherokees

Chief Bowles and the Texas Cherokees

by
Mary Whatley Clarke

NORMAN
UNIVERSITY OF OKLAHOMA PRESS

By Mary Whatley Clarke

The Palo Pinto Story (Fort Worth, 1956)
(ed.) *Life in the Saddle,* by Frank Collinson (Norman, 1963)
David G. Burnet: First President of Texas (Austin, 1969)
Thomas J. Rusk: Soldier, Statesman, Jurist (Austin, 1971)
Chief Bowles and the Texas Cherokees (Norman, 1971)

Chief Bowles and the Texas Cherokees is Volume 113
in The Civilization of the American Indian Series.

ISBN: 978-0-8061-3436-9 (paper)

Library of Congress Catalog Card Number: 72-160490

Copyright © 1971 by the University of Oklahoma Press, Publishing
Division of the University. Manufactured in the U.S.A.
First paperback printing 2002.

In loving memory
of my great-grandmother,
Mary B. Lasater Whatley Phillips,
whose dark eyes and olive skin were
inherited from a Cherokee ancestor

Foreword

During my research on another book about early Texas, I often came upon the name "Chief Bowles" or "the Bowl." Who was he and what part had he played in Texas history? I learned that, while accounts of his tragic role in the Indian history of Texas appeared here and there, no one had succeeded in assembling all available information about him in a single work. His impact on the history of Texas was, in my opinion, sufficiently important to justify a book about him. Furthermore, I felt that Chief Bowles and his people, whose bones have rested under the tall pines of East Texas for a century and a half, should not be forgotten. Thus this work was begun.

At a family reunion in Georgia several years ago I discovered quite by accident that my paternal great-grandmother had Cherokee blood. This discovery triggered my already lively curiosity about Chief Bowles and the Texas Cherokees and inspired me to complete this book.

It is my hope that, with this addition to the recorded Indian history of Texas, I have honored the memory of Chief Bowles. He was not a savage redskin bent on killing the white man, as a few writers would have you believe. (Those writers are in the minority; more historians have praised than condemned him.) He and his tribe undoubtedly enjoyed the highest state of civilization of all the Indians who ever lived in Texas. I trust that my readers will view Chief Bowles in the sympathetic light that he well deserves.

MARY WHATLEY CLARKE

Fort Worth, Texas
January 19, 1971

Acknowledgments

This work could not have been completed without the generous help of librarians and other individuals. I am sincerely grateful to the following persons: Mary Faris and Joanween Gill, librarians of Texas Christian University, Fort Worth; Mrs. Alene Simpson, librarian, and Mrs. Rella Looney, Indian Archives Division, Oklahoma Historical Society, Oklahoma City; Mrs. H. H. Keene, Thomas Gilcrease Institute of American History and Art, Tulsa; Mrs. Alice Timmons, Frank Phillips Collection, University of Oklahoma, Norman, and Jack Haley, assistant curator, Western History Collections, University of Oklahoma, who with his staff made an intensive search for references to Chief Bowles in the Cherokee Nation Papers; John L. Ferguson, state historian, Arkansas History Commission, Little Rock, who examined the card files of the Biographical Index for references to Chief Bowles; Roy P. Basler, chief, the Library of Congress, Washington, D.C., who searched in the manuscript division, as well as in the indexes to the Andrew Jackson and Martin Van Buren Papers for Bowles data; Matt P. Lowman II, of the Newberry Library, Chicago, for searching the John Howard Payne Papers for Bowles references; attorney Jenkins Garrett, Fort Worth, who gave me access to his private library; Malcolm McLean, of Texas Christian University, who guided me to several interesting Bowles references from the Sterling P.

Robertson Papers, which he is editing; William C. Sturtevant, Office of Anthropology, Smithsonian Institution, Washington, D.C., who furnished a helpful list of Bowles references; Morris S. Burton, Tyler, and R. F. Moore, Jacksonville, who provided photographs; T. L. Ballenger, history professor emeritus in Northeastern Oklahoma State College, Tahlequah, who took me to see the sword that Sam Houston presented to Bowles, now a treasured relic in the Tahlequah Masonic Lodge.

Texas Assistant Attorney General Alan Minter, Austin, has my gratitude for sending me the latest brief regarding Cherokee claims in Texas. Mildred Wyatt, director of the East Texas Collection, Paul L. Boynton Library, Stephen F. Austin State University, Nacogdoches, Texas, is affectionately remembered for her many kindnesses.

Four historians, Ernest W. Winkler, Albert Woldert, Dorman H. Winfrey, and James Mooney, wrote articles on the Texas Cherokees and Chief Bowles which helped greatly in my research. Emmet Starr's book *History of the Cherokee Indians, Their Legends and Folklore* was particularly helpful. John H. Reagan, a contemporary of Chief Bowles, paints the best word picture of the Cherokee leader in his *Memoirs*.

Lastly, I am deeply grateful to Mrs. Cecil B. Williams, associate professor of English in Texas Christian University, and to my husband, Joe A. Clarke, who provided invaluable editorial assistance.

Contents

Illustrations

Maps

Chief Bowles and the Texas Cherokees

CHAPTER I

Chief Bowles and His People Go to Texas

> Can a tree that is torn from its root by the fountain,
> The pride of the valley, green, spreading and fair,
> Can it flourish, removed to the rock of the mountain,
> Unwarmed by the sun and unwatered by care.
>
> John Howard Payne[1]

A PLOWED-UP arrow in a cornfield, an occasional Indian mound in the shadow of the forest, a creek named Bowl, and a town and a county named Cherokee are poignant reminders of old Chief Bowles and his Cherokee people, who claimed a large area of East Texas as their particular paradise from 1819 to 1839. More than 130 years have passed since the remnant of this historic tribe of red men was driven out of Texas to begin a tragic pilgrimage across Red River into Indian Territory, now Oklahoma. The rich, forested lands of pine, sweet gum, and red oak that held the bones of their people were left for the white man to fight over. The Texas Cherokee saga had come to an end. Gone were their council houses, the cool springs, and the familiar trails. Their forced trek was one of tears and lamentations. Grant Foreman, a sympathetic historian, wrote in his book *Indian Removal*:

> It is doubtful if white people with their readier adaptability can understand the sense of grief and desolation that overwhelmed the Indians when they were forced to leave their homes and all they loved behind. . . . They cherished the earth that held the bones of their ancestors more than white people did. . . . Their loss was cataclysmic.[2]

[1] Emmet Starr, *History of the Cherokee Indians, Their Legends and Folklore*, 34. Hereafter cited as *History of the Cherokee Indians*.

[2] Grant Foreman, *Indian Removal: The Emigration of the Five Civilized Tribes of Indians*, 9. Hereafter cited as *Indian Removal*.

The Texas Cherokees were a branch of the old Cherokee Nation who had lived in their ancestral homes in the southeastern United States from time immemorial. The word Cherokee was derived from two words, *a-che-la* ("fire") and *ah-gi* ("he takes"). The Cherokees worshiped the sun as their deity and called him "the apportioner" because he had given them their sacred fire, which they kept burning day and night and to which their priests offered sacrifice. He also divided time into day and night and gave them the four seasons.[3]

When the first white men ventured into the Cherokee country, the Cherokees had sixty-four towns and villages and about six thousand fighting men, "defended by blue-topped ledges of inaccessible mountains; where but three of them could make a successful campaign, even against their own red-colored enemies."[4]

The Cherokees called themselves Aniyunwiya, "the principal people." Their language revealed their Iroquoian ancestry, and their Algonquin-given name, Allegewi, pointed to Pennsylvania as their home. Delaware traditions pictured their movement to the South as a tribal expulsion punishing a treacherous attack on a Delaware ally. After continuous warfare the tribe finally halted in North Carolina and founded their main town, which they called Cuttawa (Bryson City).[5]

The Cherokees were considered the mountaineers of the South and held the entire Allegheny region as their own. That great expanse of country comprised an area of approximately forty thousand square miles. Today it would include parts of Virginia, Tennessee, North and South Carolina, Georgia, and Alabama. It stretched from the interlocking headstreams of the Kanawha and Tennessee rivers southward almost to the site of Atlanta,

---

[3] Albert Woldert, "The Last of the Cherokees in Texas, and the Life and Death of Chief Bowles," *Chronicles of Oklahoma*, Vol. I, No. 2 (1921–23), 179–226. Hereafter cited as "The Last of the Cherokees in Texas."

[4] Samuel Cole Williams, *Adair's History of the American Indians*, 238.

[5] R. S. Cotterill, *The Southern Indians: The Story of the Civilized Tribes Before Removal*, 5–6. Hereafter cited as *The Southern Indians*.

Georgia. It reached from the Blue Ridge on the east to the Cumberland range on the west.[6] The musical-sounding, present-day names of towns, streams, and mountains in this area recall the ancient Cherokee inhabitants.

The Cherokees said that the great buzzard, grandfather of all the later buzzards, created the beautiful valleys and mountains in the Allegheny region. When the earth was flat and still soft, the great buzzard flew over the country. He became tired, and his flapping wings dragged the ground, creating great valleys. When he turned them upward to fly again, mountains grew. Thus, they said, were formed the valleys and mountains so well loved by the Cherokees.[7]

The white settlers wanted the Cherokee land, and President Andrew Jackson signed the removal act which resulted in the long, heartbreaking trek in 1838–39.[8] As a result of this act, most of the Cherokees living east of the Mississippi River, especially those in Georgia, were forced to leave the land of their fathers and migrate to an unknown region, then known as Indian Territory, in present Oklahoma. Terrible hardships were suffered on that long journey. Thousands died. It has since been called the Trail of Tears.[9] Never was a migration in America more tragic, not even that of the Acadians.[10]

When old Chief Junaluska of the Cherokees saw the misery and heartbreak of his people, he recalled that, twenty-five years earlier, on March 29, 1814, he had saved Andrew Jackson's life

[6] James Mooney, *Myths of the Cherokee*, Bureau of American Ethnology *Nineteenth Annual Report*, Pt. I, 14.

[7] John P. Brown, *Old Frontiers: The Story of the Cherokee Indians from Earliest Times to the Dates of Their Removal to the West, 1838*, 17. Hereafter cited as *Old Frontiers*.

[8] Grace Steele Woodward, *The Cherokees*, 218.

[9] A play entitled "The Trail of Tears," written by Kermit Hunter, was first presented in the summer of 1969 in a large, open-air theater at Tsa-La-Gi, the Cherokee village near Tahlequah, Oklahoma. Many of the persons in the cast are part Cherokee. This annual presentation by Hunter is a continuation of his well-known drama about the Cherokees, "Unto These Hills," which is presented during the summer months in Cherokee, North Carolina.

[10] Mooney, *Myths of the Cherokee*, Pt. I, 130.

at Horseshoe Bend. He had plunged his steel tomahawk into the skull of a Creek Indian who had attacked the general. Junaluska and five hundred of his bravest warriors and scouts had helped Jackson win that historic battle. Now, seeing his people forced from their ancestral domain, he said with tears in his eyes, "If I had known that Jackson would drive us from our homes I would have killed him that day at the Horse Shoe."[11]

When the Cherokees migrated west, they had already advanced along the road to civilization. Sequoyah had evolved a syllabary, and many of the tribe could read and write.[12] Thus the sacred formulas and early history of their race were preserved in writing. The Bible had been translated and published in Cherokee, but many felt as old Chief Drowning Bear did about the greedy whites who coveted their lands. After listening to biblical passages read in Cherokee, he said, "It seems a good book but it is strange that the white man who has heard it so long is no better."[13]

Today there is an eastern band of Cherokees living on the Qualla Boundary in western North Carolina. Grace Steele Woodward described them in her book *The Cherokees*:

> These ancestors . . . were the little frenzied band of Cherokees who, eluding the military in 1838, hid for several years in North Carolina caves and mountains adjacent to the site of the present Qualla Boundary, subsisting on roots, berries, and the wildlife around them.[14]

James Mooney wrote that this band was joined by others who had managed to break through the guard at collecting stations, until the number in hiding amounted to 1,000 or more.[15] These Cherokees now number about 4,500 persons. Today there are

[11] Rachel Caroline Eaton, *John Ross and the Cherokee Indians*, 26; Irvin M. Peithmann, *Red Men of Fire*, 52.

[12] Brown, *Old Frontiers*, 489–90.

[13] Mrs. B. J. Bandy, "Old Van House," *Chronicles of Oklahoma*, Vol. XXXII, No. 1 (1954), 94.

[14] P. 12

[15] *Myths of the Cherokee*, Pt. I, 157.

approximately 100,000 Cherokee mixed-bloods. Of this number 47,000 live in Oklahoma.[16] Earl Boyd Pierce, of Muskogee, Oklahoma, general counsel of the Cherokee Nation, says that of this number probably from 1,000 to 1,500 are descendants of the Texas Cherokees.

The Bowl (Diwa'li,[17] or Chief Bowles)[18] was born in North Carolina about 1756.[19] It is thought that his father was a Scotch-Irish trader and his mother a Cherokee, but no one really knows. Mooney wrote that the Cherokees' advance in civilization was due to intermarriage of their women with white men who were mostly traders of good stock and not the "Squaw Man type." He believed that the families making Cherokee history were nearly all of mixed blood.[20]

Years later, John H. Reagan, who first met Bowles when the chief was eighty-three years old, was convinced that white blood ran through the Bowl's veins.[21] When visiting with Bowles before the Texas Cherokee War, he noticed with interest the Anglo characteristics of the Indian chief. Bowles had an "Eng-

[16] Woodward, *The Cherokees*, 9–14.

[17] Frederick Webb Hodge (ed.), *Handbook of American Indians North of Mexico*, Bureau of American Ethnology *Bulletin No. 30*, Vol. I, 163.

[18] Not to be confused with William Augustus Bowles, Anglo adventurer of Frederick County, Maryland. Casual readers of history are inclined to confuse the two men since they were contemporaries bearing the same name and both played significant roles in the history of the Southern Indians. William Augustus Bowles went to Florida in 1788 and with the consent of the Creek and Seminole Indians set up an Indian state called Muscogee and made himself director-general. Cotterill, *The Southern Indians*, 127–28. According to an article about William Augustus Bowles in the *Leeds* (England) *Intelligencer* of March 8, 1791: "A gentleman of fortune born in America . . . has lately attached himself to a female savage . . . has relinquished his own country . . . and adopted the manners of the virtuous though uncultivated Indian." William Augustus Bowles's date of birth has been established as 1763. The *Dictionary of American Biography* says that he died in 1805 and adds, erroneously, I believe, that Chief Bowles, friend of Sam Houston, was one of his descendants. Chief Bowles's birth date was established by his own statement in the year 1839 (see Chapter IX). He said then that he was eighty-three years of age. That would place his birth in 1756, seven years before the birth of his contemporary, William Augustus Bowles. He was not, therefore, a descendant of that gentleman, and was probably not related to him in any manner.

[19] Woldert, "The Last of the Cherokees in Texas," *loc. cit.*, 187.

[20] *Myths of the Cherokee*, 83.

[21] John H. Reagan, *Memoirs* (ed. by Walter F. McCaleb), 29–30.

lish" head, sandy hair, and gray eyes. In every other way he was Indian.

It is said that Bowles's father was killed by settlers from a North Carolina settlement when Bowles was a young boy and that the vengeful son killed his father's murderers when he was fourteen years old. After that time, he hated any white person from North Carolina.[22]

After Chief Bowles's death Reagan met a commission merchant from Shreveport, Louisiana, named Bowles, who was convinced that the dead chief was his relative. Before the Revolutionary War the merchant's forebears had lived in Georgia. They were all killed by the Cherokees, with the exception of a small boy, who was carried into captivity and reared in the tribe. The Shreveport merchant was certain that Chief Bowles was that little boy grown to manhood.[23] He may well have been.

As far as is known, the Bowl made his entrance into recorded history in 1792. Dragging Canoe, known as "the savage Napoleon,"[24] chief of the Chickamauga Cherokees, died in the spring of that year in the town of Running Water, on the Tennessee River. He was succeeded as town chief by John Bowles, "an auburn haired, blue eyed half blood Scottish Cherokee about thirty-two years of age."[25]

Running Water was one of the Five Lower Towns at the base of Chattanooga (Lookout) Mountain. It was situated below the present Hale's Bar Lock and Dam in the state of Tennessee. Lookout Town, on the east side of Lookout Creek, became the rendezvous for many Cherokee chiefs. Bowles was one of them. All of them hated the whites.[26]

The Five Lower Towns became the most formidable bastion in the Cherokee domain, and the inhabitants became known "not only for their disposition to commit injuries on the citizens

[22] Woldert, "The Last of the Cherokees in Texas," *loc. cit.*, 187–88.
[23] Reagan, *Memoirs*, 29–30.
[24] Brown, *Old Frontiers*, 175.
[25] Starr, *History of the Cherokee Indians*, 35.
[26] Woodward, *The Cherokees*, 100–101.

of the United States, but from their ability to perform them."[27]

The Bowl was in the prime of manhood when he became town chief of Running Water. One can picture him, handsome and proud, full of strength, tall and erect, shrewd, intelligent, and always wary where white settlers were concerned.

According to John Haywood, who wrote a history of Tennessee in 1823, a boat owned by William Scott left Knoxville for Natchez in 1794. Besides Scott, five other men, three women, four children, and twenty Negro slaves were on board. The boat was loaded with valuable merchandise. As the boat passed down the Tennessee River, it was fired upon by the Cherokees at Running Water and Long Island villages. The whites were not injured, but they returned the fire and wounded two Indians. One hundred and fifty Indians then gathered and pursued the boat to Muscle Shoals, where it was overtaken. The Indians killed all the white people, plundered the boat, and took the Negroes as captives.[28]

The Reverend Cephas Washburn, an early missionary to the Cherokees,[29] tells an entirely different version of the massacre in his book, *Reminiscences of the Indians*.[30] Washburn recalled that a treaty had been made between the Cherokees and the United States government in 1785. In that treaty the Cherokees had given up some of their land, for which they were to be paid cer-

[27] Governor Blount to Secretary of War, January 14, 1793, *Territorial Papers of the United States* (ed. by Clarence Edwin Carter), IV, 227.

[28] John Haywood, *The Natural and Aboriginal History of Tennessee up to the First Settlements Therein by the White People in the Year 1768*, 322. Hereafter cited as *History of Tennessee*. In the Grant Foreman Papers in the Thomas Gilcrease Institute of History and Art, Tulsa, there is a manuscript entitled "The Bowle." Foreman had copied it from *American State Papers*, XIX, 309. It agrees with Haywood's account but names Bowles as the leader of the attack.

[29] Washburn lived among the Indians for many years. In 1821 he conducted the first services in Dwight Mission, on the west side of Illinois Bayou near the site of the present Russellville, Arkansas. The mission was named for Timothy Dwight, a former president of Yale College, and was built especially for the Cherokee Indians. Grant Foreman, "Dwight Mission," *Chronicles of Oklahoma*, Vol. XII (March–December, 1934). There is no doubt that Washburn told the story of the Indians as he heard it, but some historians, such as Moody, did not fully credit his version.

[30] Cephas Washburn, *Reminiscences of the Indians*, ed. by Hugh Park, 59–65.

tain sums of money. The Cherokees from across their nation went to Tellico Blockhouse in Eastern Tennessee, where they received the money. At one of those meetings, in the late winter of 1793 or the early part of 1794, the Indians gathered, received their money from the government, and after a peaceful and harmonious meeting returned to their villages.

One group of the Chickamauga Cherokees, of which Bowles was a member, stopped to rest and hunt along the bank of the Tennessee River near the upper end of Muscle Shoals. While the Indians were encamped there, several boats carrying emigrants bound for Louisiana came down the river and stopped at the head of the Shoals. Scott and Stewart, who were among the men on the boats, had a supply of goods which they wanted to trade to the Indians as they passed through their territory.

The white men soon learned that the Cherokees had real money and invited them on board the boats, where the Indians were treated to as much whisky as they could drink. Soon most of the warriors were drunk. They were shown the glittering, tawdry wares of the white traders. The Indians eagerly bought glass beads at twelve dollars a strand and mirrors for sixteen dollars and paid as much as thirty dollars an ounce for body paint. The trading stopped when the money was gone.

Washburn wrote that, after sobering up, Bowles and his warriors realized that they had been the dupes of the white men. Bowles then took the merchandise back to the boats and offered to pay four dollars a gallon for the whisky if the traders would refund the rest of their money. Bowles was ordered off the boat, and his request was refused. The warriors wanted immediate revenge, but Bowles realized the wisdom of a peaceful settlement. Taking two of his more composed warriors with him, he again returned to the boats, warning the traders that the Indians would fight if their money was not returned. Stewart and Scott, seizing boat poles, attacked the three Indians. Stewart plunged the iron socket of his pole into an Indian's breast and killed him. Another Cherokee was knocked down by Stewart's pole and was thrown into the river. The Bowl escaped but soon returned with his warriors. They fired upon Stewart and Scott, who were killed instantly. Then the Cherokees killed the remaining white men in the boats. They did not harm the women and children nor the slaves.

Washburn related that he later met one of the captured women in New Orleans and wrote that she was truly "a mother of Israel." She told him the particulars of the massacre and spoke of the kindness shown all the white ladies and children by Chief Bowles and his party.

Afraid of what his tribe would think about the massacre, since the Cherokee Indians were supposed to be abiding by a treaty of amity with the whites, Bowles and his band headed down the Tennessee River in the boats, taking the women and children, slaves, and booty with them. They traversed the Ohio and Mississippi rivers to the mouth of the St. Francis River in present Missouri.[31]

After arriving at the St. Francis, Bowles ordered his warriors to put the women and children in boats and send them downriver to New Orleans. He gave each woman a slave and sent four strong black men to look after them. He provided them with food and gave them what personal belongings they could take.[32]

Bowles and his warriors then continued up the St. Francis to await results. The Cherokees on the Tennessee went into council immediately after the massacre and drew up a memorial to the United States government stating that they had had nothing to do with the killings. They placed the entire blame on Bowles and his followers and disowned the group. They said that they were abiding by the treaty with the government and would help find and arrest Bowles.

When Bowles learned that he was in disfavor with many of the Chickamauga Cherokees, he decided to make his home in the French territory of Missouri. He liked the climate there.

[31] *Ibid.*
[32] *Ibid.*

Game was plentiful, and he felt that the French would protect him and his followers. He settled on the St. Francis and made it his home for several years. In time other Cherokees joined him there.[33]

Washburn concluded his narrative by saying that the whole matter of the massacre was investigated by the government of the United States and that the Cherokees were fully justified. According to Washburn the property was confiscated and declared by treaty to belong justly to the perpetrators of the Muscle Shoals Massacre.[34]

Mooney wrote that Washburn's statement contained several errors. The annuity at that time amounted to fifteen hundred dollars for the tribe, less than ten cents a head. That would not have been enough for the Indians to pay such high prices for beads, mirrors and other trinkets. Mooney admitted, however, that it was possible that the whites might have provoked the attack, a conclusion reached by the missionary since he had heard the story from one of the women in the party. This was proof that not all the whites had been killed, as recorded by Haywood and

---

[33] *Ibid.*

[34] *Ibid.* Perhaps Washburn based his statement on the verdict handed down by the Claims Committee of the United States government to the heirs of William Scott and James and John Pettigrew. On January 22, 1805, about ten and a half years after the Muscle Shoals Massacre, Alexander Scott, a nephew of William Scott and a citizen of Williamsburg, South Carolina, sought indemnity from the United States government for Indian depredations against his late uncle and James and John Pettigrew. Scott was acting as agent for the parties concerned. He said that William Scott and the Pettigrew brothers left South Carolina in February, 1794, for Natchez. They took twenty-one Negroes with them and goods and chattels valued at more than one thousand dollars. They were attacked about June 9, 1794, by the Cherokee Indians at Muscle Shoals. All the white people were put to death, and the Negroes, goods, and chattels were carried away. The petitioner solicited relief from the United States government. Scott's petition was handled by a man named Dana of the Committee of Claims. No indemnity was awarded because "the committee do not consider the United States bound to guaranty the possession of Negro slaves to individuals passing for no public purpose through the country of hostile savages." (At that time Muscle Shoals lay within a tract which had not been relinquished or ceded by the Indians to the United States.) "Indemnity for Indian Depredations," *American State Papers*, No. 160, Class IX, Claims.

others. Mooney concluded that it was probable that only the white men had been killed.[35]

Chief Bowles and his people lived in the valley of the St. Francis in southeastern Missouri until 1811. During that year a violent earthquake produced tremors and oscillations in the earth.[36] The ground shook and sank in many places.[37] The Cherokees were badly frightened and thought the Great Spirit was warning them to move from that country. As a result the tribe moved into the territory between the Arkansas and White rivers in present-day Arkansas. The region was virgin hunting ground and was far removed from white settlers. Other Cherokees began to emigrate to Arkansas, and by 1813 perhaps one-third of the Eastern Cherokees were living west of the Mississippi.[38]

Chief Bowles's settlement was near the mouth of Petit Jean Creek, about four miles from the Arkansas River, in what is now Conway County, about ten miles northwest of present Perryville.[39] The tribe lived there until a survey was made of the Cherokee Nation of Arkansas by the United States in 1819.[40] Since Bowles's village was not a part of the land ceded to the Cherokees by the United States government, his tribe had to move.[41]

[35] *Myths of the Cherokee*, 101.

[36] Starr, *History of the Cherokee Indians*, 38–39.

[37] Blake Clark, "America's Greatest Earthquake," *Reader's Digest*, April, 1969. The main tremor, which occurred in 1811, was felt near New Madrid, Missouri, but frightened Indians living as far north as Canada. Houses, trees, and people were lifted from the earth and thrown down like toys. Entire forests fell. The Mississippi River flowed backward for over one mile. It is no wonder that the Cherokees thought the Great Spirit was angry.

[38] Starr, *History of the Cherokee Indians*, 38–39.

[39] Woldert, "The Last of the Cherokees in Texas," *loc. cit.*, 189.

[40] Starr, *History of the Cherokee Indians*, 87.

[41] *Ibid.* Bowles had probably been warned to leave by the Cherokee chief in the stipulated reservation in Arkansas. A letter sent by Secretary of War John C. Calhoun about that time to the chief stated that some of the Cherokees had improperly settled south of the Arkansas River on United States lands, outside the Cherokee treaty lands, and that the chief must immediately order the people to move into the limits of the reservation. Letters Sent, Indian Affairs, War Department, Secretary's Office. Vol. E (August 3, 1820–October 25, 1825), 167–384.

After leaving their home on Petit Jean Creek, Bowles and his people probably moved to Lost Prairie, Arkansas, on the west bank of Red River, in what is now Miller County. That location was about twenty miles east of the present city of Texarkana, Arkansas.[42] Bowles later told Indian Agent Martin Lacy and John H. Reagan that he and his people had stopped there a short while before moving into Texas.[43]

During their sojourn on Lost Prairie, Chief Bowles and his warriors no doubt ventured into Texas to hunt. They liked what they saw, and Bowles made plans to move his people to that country. He had lived peacefully under the French in Missouri and believed he could live in peace under the Spanish government in Texas.

During the winter of 1819–20, Chief Bowles, with sixty of his men and their families, moved into Texas and settled in Caddo Indian country.[44] Bowles later told Indian Agent Lacy that his people had first lived on the Three Forks of the Trinity (now Dallas, Texas),[45] but the prairie Indians had forced them to settle near Spanish Fort (Nacogdoches).[46] Bowles established his village about fifty miles north of Nacogdoches.[47]

Albert Woldert, author of "The Last of the Cherokees in Texas," spent perhaps as much time as any historian in determining the sites of Chief Bowles's villages in the Cherokee Nation of Texas. In 1923, Woldert visited the Cherokee country and interviewed many old-timers in the area. Some of them had

---

[42] Woldert, "The Last of the Cherokees in Texas," loc. cit., 190.

[43] Reagan, Memoirs, 29–36.

[44] Ernest William Winkler, "The Cherokee Indians in Texas," Quarterly of the Texas State Historical Association, Vol. VII, No. 1 (July, 1903–April, 1904), 96.

[45] On July 18, 1969, W. W. Keeler, of Bartlesville, Oklahoma, principal chief of the Cherokee Nation, unveiled a historical marker overlooking the R. L. Thornton Freeway in Dallas, commemorating the settlement of Chief Bowles and ninety members of the Cherokee Nation in the Dallas area in 1819. The Cherokees are considered to be the first immigrants in the Dallas area from the United States. Dallas Morning News, July 19, 1969.

[46] Reagan, Memoirs, 29–36.

[47] Hubert Howe Bancroft, History of the North Mexican States and Texas, XVI, 103–104n.

been living there a half century or more. With their help, and that of a Texas map dated 1835–36, he was able to determine Bowles's first village, north of Nacogdoches.[48] It was in the William Ravy survey on Caney Creek, Rusk County, about nine miles north of Henderson, Texas. It was probably the best-known and most stationary Cherokee village ever established in Texas.[49] Houston sent mail to Chief Bowles at this village in 1835, though he later addressed the chief in care of the Cherokee Nation.[50] No doubt this was the village visited by Houston and Forbes in February, 1836, when the treaty with Chief Bowles was signed (see Chapter VI).

Pioneer settlers pointed out the site of another Cherokee village to Woldert. This village was on the Pru league, along the east side of Bowles Creek where it flows through the old Blackwell property east of Arp, Texas. The remains of a peach orchard, planted by the Cherokees, was still standing. Joe White, a resident in the vicinity, told Woldert that just before his grandfather, Jesse Chambers, came to Texas in 1835, he met Chief Bowles in Shreveport, Louisiana. The chief was selling lead which he carried by pack train. It was thought that a stone ruin still standing along Bowles Creek had been used as a smelter.[51]

Whether the Spanish government had given Chief Bowles permission to move into Texas is debatable. Mirabeau B. Lamar wrote:

> It was obvious from a cursory examination of their history that the immigrant tribes from the United States had no legal or equitable claim to any portion of our territory ... that their immigration to Texas was unsolicited and unauthorized.[52]

[48] Woldert, "The Last of the Cherokees in Texas," *loc. cit.*, 192–93.

[49] Woldert added some typed sheets to his article after it was published and included them in a bound volume which he gave to George Crocket, of Nacogdoches. In those pages he stated more definitely where Bowles's village had been situated and said that old Indian carvings on near-by trees could still be distinctly seen. They included turtles, an alligator, a snake, a diamond, and the head of a chief in feathered headdress.

[50] Woldert, "The Last of the Cherokees in Texas," *loc. cit.*, 192–93.

[51] *Ibid.*, 193–95.

[52] Quoted in John Henry Brown, *History of Texas from 1685 to 1892*, II, 153.

Mooney wrote that many Cherokee Indians had fought with the British during the Revolutionary War and afterward had applied to the Spanish government at New Orleans in 1782 for permission to settle on the west side of the Mississippi in Spanish Territory. They had been given permission to do so. Whether that ruling applied to Texas when Bowles led his people into that territory is not known.[53] Emmet Starr wrote that a representative of the dominion of Spain had promised Bowles and his people land in the province of Texas on the Sabine River, extending from the Angelina River to the Trinity.[54]

The Cherokees were the first tribe of civilized Indians to go to Texas.[55] Thomas Nuttall, the naturalist, saw some of the Western Cherokees along the Arkansas River in 1819 about the time Bowles and his tribe went to Texas. Nuttall said that both banks of the river were lined with the Indians' houses and fences, and that the homes were decently furnished and the farms well fenced and stocked. "We perceive a happy approach toward civilization," he wrote.[56]

The Cherokees loved their new home in Texas. They did not feel crowded by white settlers. At that time no more than seven thousand American colonists lived in the province of Texas. There were about one hundred thousand head of cattle and forty

53 Mooney, *Myths of the Cherokee*, Pt. I, 101.
54 Starr, *History of the Cherokee Indians*, 187.
55 Woldert, "The Last of the Cherokees in Texas," *loc. cit.*, 181.
56 Starr, *History of the Cherokee Indians*, 39. The *Arkansas Gazette* (Little Rock), April 15, 1830, carried a letter from the secretary of war to the United States Congress about the advancement of the Cherokees: "While many of the Indian tribes have acquired only the vices with which a savage people usually become tainted by their intercourse with those who are civilized; others appear to be making gradual advance in industry and civilization. Among them may be placed the Cherokees. . . . The Cherokees exhibit a more favorable appearance than any other tribe of Indians. There are already established schools among them. There are about one hundred youths of both sexes in school. Besides reading, writing and arithmetic, the boys are taught agriculture and mechanical arts and the girls are taught sewing, knitting and weaving." The May 26, 1821, *Gazette* carried the following quote from a missionary: "It no longer remains a doubt whether the Cherokees of America can be civilized. The Cherokees have gone too far in the pleasant path of civilization to return to the rough and unbeaten track of savage life."

or fifty thousand head of horses in the province.[57] The Cherokees built their tipis beneath the tall pines and cleared patches of the forest to plant their corn. Buffalo meat was plentiful. They dried the meat in thin strips and ate it with *soffica,* a hominy made from corn.[58] The streams were full of fish. Natural springs furnished clear, cold water. They hoped to make this land their home forever.

The territory they claimed lay between the Trinity and Sabine rivers north of the San Antonio Road.[59] Today the area would include Smith and Cherokee counties, the western third of Rusk County, the southwestern fourth of Gregg County, and the eastern fourth of Van Zandt County.[60]

In time the Texas Cherokees were joined by other Cherokees from the United States. The noted chief Tahchee, or Dutch, one of the first Cherokees to emigrate to Arkansas from the old Cherokee Nation east of the Mississippi, was one of them. He opposed the Treaty of 1828 and spent a few years with Chief Bowles in Texas. He led war parties against the wild tribes during his stay in Texas and later returned to the United States and continued his warfare, especially against the Osages. He finally made peace with the United States government and became a loyal scout.[61]

The Texas Cherokees formed a loose confederacy with other refugee Indians, including Shawnees, Delawares, Kickapoos, Choctaws, Biloxis, Alabamas, and Coushattas.[62] The Texas Cherokees were the largest and most important band, however, and the Bowl "was regarded as chief and principal man of them all."

[57] Winkler, "The Cherokee Indians in Texas," *loc. cit.,* 96.
[58] Woldert, "The Last of the Cherokees in Texas," *loc. cit.,* 186.
[59] Starr, *History of the Cherokee Indians,* 182.
[60] Morris S. Burton, "The Cherokee War, 1839," *Chronicles of Smith County,* Vol. V, No. 2 (Fall, 1966), 33–34.
[61] Mooney, *Myths of the Cherokee,* Pt. I, 141.
[62] *Ibid.,* 143.

CHAPTER II

Chief Richard Fields Goes to Mexico City

A<small>LTHOUGH</small> Bowles led his people into Texas, he did not remain head chief very long. He was superseded by Richard Fields, a shrewd and intelligent half-blood.[1] Perhaps this change in leadership was the result of an election, for the Cherokees had many tribal rules which they carried out systematically. According to contemporary accounts they were considered the most civilized of the Indian tribes.[2] Hugh Park wrote in the preface to the Reverend Cephas Washburn's *Reminiscences of the Indians*: "Among all the tribes that have peopled our native forests, the Cherokees, it is believed, stood preeminent."

Washburn described an Indian election which he attended.[3] He said that the Indians had a simple method of electing their chiefs which "possessed some advantages over the practice of more civilized people." A certain day was set aside for the event, and it was made known throughout the nation that a principal

[1] Dorman H. Winfrey, "Chief Bowles of the Texas Cherokee," *Chronicles of Oklahoma*, Vol. XXXII, No. 1 (1954), 31. Chief Richard Fields is not to be confused with his oldest son, Richard Fields, whom Edward Everett Dale mentions frequently in his book *Cherokee Cavaliers*. The son was a member of the delegation of Southern Cherokees who went to Washington in the summer of 1866 to make a treaty with the United States. J. J. Hill, in the index to Emmet Starr's *Old Cherokee Families*, lists Richard Fields as a son of the Cherokee chief. So does James Manford Carselowey, a Fields descendant now living in Adair, Oklahoma, who sent the information to the author.

[2] Woldert, "The Last of the Cherokees in Texas," *loc. cit.*, 187.

[3] Washburn, *Reminiscences of the Indians*, 29–30.

chief was to be elected. Qualified voters were to meet on the borders of a certain prairie, and on the day specified warriors gathered there from all directions. Two warriors, called electors, stepped in front of the multitude. Each of them called out the name of a distinguished warrior whom he thought well qualified to be the chief. The electors then called their candidates from the crowd and led them some distance away. Leaving them there, they returned to the people, and each elector made a short speech pointing out the qualifications of his candidate. They asked the voters to show their preference by forming two lines to the right and left of the speakers. Each elector counted the warriors on his side and called out the result. The winner was then presented to the warriors and proclaimed the duly elected chief.

It was customary for the chiefs to hold office for four years.[4] Thus it could have been that Bowles's term of office expired soon after the Cherokees arrived in Texas and that Fields was elected to succeed him. In view of the constant warfare and the danger of imminent death the western Cherokees customarily elected three chiefs at a time to assure a line of succession. No doubt Bowles was the second ranking chief, for he was high in the governing council and usually accompanied Chief Fields on missions to the Mexican authorities.[5]

Chief Fields realized from the beginning that the rich lands of eastern Texas where the Cherokees had settled were coveted by white settlers. For that reason he wanted to be sure that the Cherokees had a title to their land and could live there in peace and security.[6] He lost no time putting the question to James Dill, alcalde of Nacogdoches. He wrote to Dill on February 1, 1822:

> I wish to fall at your feet and humbly ask you what must be done with us poor Indians. We have some grants that were given us when we lived under the Spanish Government and we wish you to

[4] Woldert, "The Last of the Cherokees in Texas," *loc. cit.*, 187.
[5] Winkler, "The Cherokee Indians in Texas," *loc. cit.*, 102.
[6] Mexico won her independence from Spain in 1821, and from that date on the colonists had to deal with the Mexican authorities.

send us news by the next mail whether they will be reversed or not. And if we were permitted we will come as soon as possible to present ourselves before you in a manner agreeable to our talents. If we present ourselves in a rough manner we pray you to right us. Our intentions are good toward the government. Yours as chief of the Cherokee Nation. Fields. [Written by an interpreter.[7]]

The grants referred to in Fields's letter were mere permits from Spanish officials allowing the Cherokees to live in that part of the province.[8]

Fields received no answer from the alcalde, and on November 8 he set out for Bexar (San Antonio) to see José Felix Trespalacious, governor of the province of Texas, about a title to the Cherokee land. He was accompanied by Chief Bowles and about twenty other members of the tribe.[9]

Governor Trespalacious was favorably impressed with the Cherokee delegation. Although he had no authority to give them a written title to their land, he signed a treaty with Chief Fields permitting him to go to Mexico City to lay his case before His Imperial Majesty. The agreement was as follows:

Article 1st. That the said Chief Richard, with five others of his tribe, accompanied by Mr. Antonio Mexia and Antonio Wolfe, who act as interpreters, may proceed to Mexico, to treat with his Imperial Majesty, relative to the settlement which said chief wishes to make for those of his tribe who are already in the territory of Texas, and also for those who are still in the United States.

Article 2nd. That the other Indians in the city, and who do not accompany the before mentioned, will return to their village in the vicinity of Nacogdoches, and communicate to those who are at said village, the terms of this agreement.

Article 3rd. That a party of the warriors of said village must be constantly kept on the road leading from the province to the United States, to prevent stolen animals from being carried

[7] Starr, *History of the Cherokee Indians*, 192.
[8] Winkler, "The Cherokee Indians in Texas," *loc. cit.*, 99.
[9] *Ibid.*

thither, and to apprehend and punish those evil disposed foreigners, who form assemblages, and abound on the banks of the River Sabine within the Territory of Texas.

Article 4th. That the Indians who return to their town, will appoint as their chief the Indian captain called Kunetand, alias Tong Turqui, to whom a copy of this agreement will be given, for the satisfaction of those of his tribe, and in order that they may fulfill its stipulations.

Article 5th. That meanwhile and until the approval of the Supreme Government is obtained, they may cultivate their lands and sow their crops, in free and peaceful possession.

Article 6th. That the said Cherokee Indians, will become immediately subject to the laws of the Empire, as well as all others who may tread her soil, and they will also take up arms in defense of the nation, if called upon to do so.

Article 7th. That they shall be considered Hispano-Americans, and entitled to all the rights and privileges granted to such; and to the same protection, should it become necessary.

Article 8th. That they can immediately commence trade with the other inhabitants of the province, and with the exception of arms and ammunitions of war, with the tribes of savages who may not be friendly to us.[10]

The treaty was signed at Bexar on November 8, 1822, by Trespalacious, José Flores, Nabor Villarreal, Richard Fields (his mark was an *X*), Baron de Bastrop, Manual Iturbi Castillo, and Franco de Castañeda.

Governor Trespalacious then dispatched an officer with the original copy of the agreement to Caspar López, commandant of the Eastern Internal Province at Saltillo. Fields and six of his warriors, including Bowles, accompanied the officer to Saltillo. In his letter to López, Governor Trespalacious spoke enthusiastically about the Cherokees. He said that they numbered about

[10] Record of Translations of Empresario Contracts, Texas General Land Office, 85.

one hundred warriors and two hundred women and children and that they worked for a living, made their own clothes from cotton which they wove into cloth, raised horses and cattle, and used firearms. He said that many of them understood English. He believed that they would be useful to the province.[11]

Commander López also seemed to be favorably impressed by the group of Indians. He sent them on to Mexico City to push their claim for a land title before the supreme executive power. The Cherokees arrived in the old Aztec capital early in 1823 and found themselves in the midst of a revolution. Emperor Agustín de Iturbide was overthrown, and a triumvirate of generals, Guadalupe Victoria, Nicolás Bravo, and Pedro Celestino Negrete, was installed on March 30, 1823. Fields and his chiefs applied to the new leaders for lands, and their petition was put before the Mexican congress. Since a colonization law had not yet been passed, nothing specific resulted. Chief Fields requested continuation of the allowance promised him for his support, and that request was granted. He was also promised a continuation of the rights stipulated in the treaty signed with Governor Trespalacious.[12]

Stephen F. Austin was in the Mexican capital at the same time, attempting to renew his father's colonial grant. Hayden E. Edwards, Robert Leftwich, and Green De Witt were also there, hoping to receive colonial grants. Though Chief Bowles, Chief Fields, and Chief Nicolet were prominent among the would-be title hunters, "in accordance with a natural jealousy toward strange Indians they were postponed and dismissed with some indefinite and perhaps illusory promise."[13]

In later years Hayden Edwards wrote President Mirabeau Buonaparte Lamar[14] that he was in Mexico City and met Fields

[11] Starr, *History of the Cherokee Indians*, 188–94.

[12] *Ibid.*

[13] "Compendium of Texas History," *Texas Almanac and Emigrant's Guide for 1858*, 168.

[14] *The Papers of Mirabeau Buonaparte Lamar*, III, 258. Hereafter cited as *Lamar Papers*.

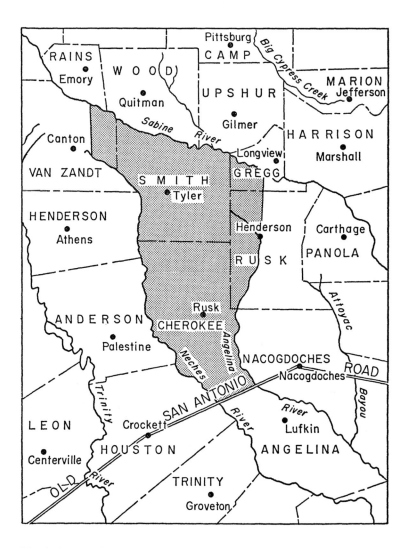

Shaded area shows the Cherokee Land Grant in Texas.

Adapted from Dorman H. Winfrey,
et al. (eds.), *Texas Indian Papers*

and Bowles there. Emperor Iturbide, he said, had paid their expenses to Mexico and had encouraged them in their plans, but his successors were not so sympathetic to the Indians. Bowles and his companions were soon out of funds and destitute. According to Edwards, he paid their expenses and was later reimbursed by the Mexican government. He said that the Cherokees wanted to remain independent and have their own laws, which the Mexican government would not permit. They wanted the Indians to enter as immigrants and become citizens of the country and members of the Catholic church. Edwards' report thus differs from the treaty signed by Fields and Trespalacious.

Lucas Alamán, minister of relations and a clever politician, dealt with the Cherokees during their stay in Mexico City. He led them to believe that their title would be more securely vested under a general colonization law. He did not give Chief Fields a written title and never planned to do so. After studying the contract made with Trespalacious, Alamán told compatriots, "It does not appear by the document that any commission or grant was made to Fields."[15]

Alamán's vague promises conciliated Fields for the time being, and the Cherokees were optimistic as they left the Mexican capital. Alamán must have known that his promises to the Cherokees could be broken at a moment's notice. He proved his deceitfulness by immediately writing to the new commandant general of the Eastern Province, Felipe de la Garza (López had been removed):

> ... be very careful and vigilant in regard to the settlement of the Cherokees ... until the publication of the General Colonization Law ... although the benefits to arise from it, cannot be extended to them.[16]

After returning to Texas, Fields wrote to the governor at Bexar that he had been granted a province sufficient for him and

---

[15] Winkler, "The Cherokee Indians in Texas," *loc. cit.*, 112.
[16] Starr, *History of the Cherokee Indians*, 190.

his people and a commission to command all the Indian tribes in the Cherokee rancheria west of the Sabine River. He would propose a peace treaty and ask the Indians to sign it. He said that he would use force of arms to subdue those who refused to sign.[17]

As time went by, Chief Fields began to feel his importance and proclaimed himself master of the Cherokee holdings. He overstepped his authority by selling land. He threatened to evict persons who did not comply with his orders. These actions put Fields in bad standing with the Mexican government.[18]

The National Colonization Law was passed on August 18, 1824, and Texas and Coahuila passed a colonization law on March 25, 1825. Many *empresarios* were granted large tracts of land in Texas on which to settle colonists. Some of the colonial grantees were Hayden E. Edwards, whom Fields and Bowles had met during their stay in Mexico City; David G. Burnet; Vincente Filisola; and Robert Leftwich. The territory granted to Edwards included the country claimed by the Cherokees.[19] Whether the authorities of Coahuila and Texas, sitting at Saltillo, purposely ignored the Cherokee rights is not known. News did not travel very fast in those days, and many settlers in Texas did not hear of the new colonization law for a long while. Whatever the circumstances, the Cherokees were the losers. They did not receive any firm titles to their land.

News of the Anglo grants deeply angered Chief Fields. His people had kept the peace. They had been good citizens long before the colonization law had been passed. They, too, deserved title to their lands. Chief Fields brooded upon their unjust treatment and decided to wreak vengeance on the Mexican government and the hated whites who would settle on the Cherokees' rich lands. Fields was further incensed by a proclamation issued on October 25, 1825, by the *empresario*, Edwards:

Whatsoever families or persons residing within the bounds of said

17 *Ibid.*, 191.
18 Woldert, "The Last of the Cherokees in Texas," *loc. cit.*, 191.
19 Starr, *History of the Cherokee Indians*, 192.

territory and all those who pretend to hold claims to any parts of the land or lands of said territory shall immediately present themselves and exhibit their titles and documents, if they have any, in order that they may be approved or rejected according to law; and if they do not do this, said land shall be sold without further question.[20]

Rumors were soon rife that Chief Fields was in league with the Comanches, Tawakonis, Wacos, and others and was planning to attack San Antonio and the new settlements. The angry chief was determined to defend his rights. He was convinced that, if the settlements grew, the government could use their militias against the Indians, that occupation of the country would destroy the game, and that the Indians would starve.[21]

Austin wrote to José Antonio Saucedo, the political chief of Coahuila and Texas, after hearing of Fields's threats. The political chief in turn wrote to the governor, asking him to send troops to Nacogdoches to check on the Indians, particularly the Cherokees, "for the various accounts of the conduct of their chief, Richard Fields, that I have received since 1824, have not won my confidence."[22] On September 28, 1825, Austin addressed the colonists: "I am creditably informed that these Indians are very much dissatisfied that their country has been given to the American *Empresarios* to be settled."[23]

Chief Fields was not as warlike in 1826. For some reason he abandoned the proposed alliance with the Comanches and other tribes and instead decided to try to obtain his land peacefully. Perhaps he was influenced to do so by a few persons with the interest of the Cherokees or Texas, or both, at heart. Chief Fields wrote the commanding officer of Texas, Mateo Ahumada, from Cherokee Town on April 22, 1825:

I shall always be ready to defend the Province in a case of trouble

[20] Winkler, "The Cherokee Indians in Texas," *loc cit.*, 117.
[21] *Ibid.*
[22] Political chief to the Governor, October 2, 1825, Blotter for 1825, Bexar Archives, Translation, Archives Collection, University of Texas Library, Austin.
[23] Winkler, "The Cherokee Indians in Texas," *loc. cit.*, 117.

. . . when able to see you will bring my papers and commission for your inspection. We have nothing to do with the Anglo Americans here and we will not submit to their laws and orders emanating from the Mexican nation. I have established laws among my people in order to live in peace and to keep them under submission to the new order of the government. . . . We employ all of our industry in the cultivation of the soil so that our works may improve every day. . . . I am happy our labors will give great satisfaction to your government. . . . In case you should be interrupted or annoyed by your subordinate neighbors let me know it, and I will at once assist you with my people, hoping reciprocity from you in case I should be oppressed. . . . There are bad men who through malice, or envy, exaggerate, lessen or pervert the truth. I do not listen to them and I am pleased that you have not listened to those who have spoken evil of me or made false reports. I expect they concern the Anglo-Americans and other white people. I desire that my people be understood at least for this year until we receive orders from the Government on the subject. I have done speaking for the present and I shall ever be your friend and brother.[24]

For the time being, Chief Fields had resolved on peace. On December 31, 1825, he and five other tribal leaders visited the alcalde in Nacogdoches and assured him of their friendship.[25]

Chief Fields wrote again to Saucedo, offering to join him in a war with the unfriendly Indians: ". . . should our government decide to wage war on these faithless savages, I hope you will have the kindness to send me a courier in order that with all my people I may go to unite with the Mexican troops and destroy this restless people who commit so many acts of hostility."[26]

Saucedo replied by thanking Fields for his offer to help fight the unfriendly Indians. He asked the Cherokee chief to send him copies of the papers permitting the Cherokees to emigrate to Texas. He said that no proof of the permits could be found in

[24] Blake Collection, Jenkins Garrett Library, Fort Worth, XI, 29–30.
[25] Winkler, "The Cherokee Indians in Texas," *loc. cit.*, 117.
[26] File 221, Nacogdoches Archives, Archives Collection, University of Texas Library, Austin.

the archives of his department or in those of the secretary of state. Such proof was needed if Fields and his people were to remain in possession of their territory.[27] Fields, however, did not produce any papers.

In the spring of 1826, Austin was ordered by Ahumada to attack the Wacos, Tawakonis, and other enemy Indians. Knowing that Chief Fields had volunteered his aid in case war was undertaken against the Comanches and their allies, Austin wrote a letter to Fields (whom he addressed as "Captain") and other chiefs and warriors of the Cherokee Nation living in Texas:

> My friends and brothers: The Mexican Government has called on the new settlers of this colony to fight their enemies, the Wacos, Tawakonis and Toweass Indians. . . . My plan is for the militia of this colony to attack the Waco and Tawakany villages on the main Brazos River at daylight on the 25th of May and for the Cherokees, Shawnees and Delawares to attack the Tawakany village on the head of the Navisota about thirty miles east of the Brazos at the same moment. . . . My friends, I have informed you of my plans . . . I have placed great confidence in you, for you are the only persons out of this colony that I have called on for aid. . . . I am the friend of the Cherokees and wish to give them an opportunity of showing the Government what good soldiers and faithful citizens they will make, and I have no doubt if you turn out in this expedition and destroy the Tawakany villages on the head of the Navisota that it will be the means of securing you land in the country for as many of your nation as wish to remove here. I have no authority to promise you land, but I will promise my aid and friendship in your favor with the Government and I have no doubt of succeeding, but you must first show the Government that you are both able and willing to fight for them.[28]

Chief Fields and Chief Bowles sent Austin a reply by the same courier who had brought Austin's letter to them. They expressed their willingness to help the colonists in such a war but said that

[27] Political chief to Richard Fields, May 3, 1826, Blotter for 1826, Bexar Archives, *loc. cit.*

[28] *The Austin Papers*, ed. by Eugene C. Barker, II, 1307.

they could not leave because of flooded rivers and creeks and because their crops were late.[29]

Mateo Ahumada, the commander of Texas, issued an order on May 4, postponing the proposed Indian attack. When Austin told him that he had asked the Cherokee chiefs to help in such an attack, Ahumada replied:

> In my opinion there is no need of our employing the Cherokees and other peaceable Indians for the purpose you propose; because, it is best that all the Indians should believe that we are not in need of them at all and that we excel them in war.[30]

No doubt Saucedo had advised Ahumada not to call on the Cherokees for aid because Fields had not produced the requested papers showing his permit of entry into Texas. The department had not yet ascertained the exact status of the Cherokees in the territory.

A few months later Fields was granted permission to attack the Indians whom Austin had proposed to fight, because they had killed some of the Cherokees.[31] Before Chief Fields and his warriors departed on that warring mission, John Dunn Hunter reached the Cherokee village. He was to wield great influence over Chief Fields.

[29] Austin to Mateo Ahumada, May 18, 1826, Bexar Archives, *loc. cit.*
[30] Commander of Texas to Austin, May 18, 1826, Bexar Archives, *loc. cit.*
[31] Richard Fields to Samuel Norris, August 26, and to Austin, August 27, 1826, Files 209 and 197, Nacogdoches Archives, *loc. cit.*

CHAPTER III

John Dunn Hunter Arrives at the Cherokee Village

In 1825 the enigmatic John Dunn Hunter entered the Cherokee village.[1] He was destined to play a tragic part in the Anglo-Mexican-Cherokee history of Texas. Many journalists in the United States accused him of being an adventurer and impostor. Others did not see him in such a light, believing that he had incurred the enmity of many persons because of his outspoken defense of the Indians.[2] Hunter was either the first philanthropist to set foot on Texas soil or one of the shrewdest schemers ever to enter the Mexican province.

In 1823, Hunter had published in Philadelphia a narrative of his life, *Manners and Customs of Several Indian Tribes Located West of the Mississippi*.[3] The work was reprinted the same year in London under the title *Memoirs of a Captivity Among the Indians of North America, from Childhood to the Age of Nineteen*. The appearance of a third edition in London shortly afterward is evidence of the popularity of the book.

Hubert Howe Bancroft wrote in his *History of the North Mexican States and Texas* that Hunter did not remember his parents, whom he believed to have been killed when he was captured, and that he did not know when or where the tragedy

[1] Henry Stuart Foote, *Texas and the Texans*, I, 240.
[2] Bancroft, *History of North Mexican States and Texas*, XVI, 103–104n.
[3] *Ibid.*

had occurred. His skill at hunting during his boyhood had been much admired by the Indians, who had given him the name Hunter, which he had since adopted as his surname. He had named himself John Dunn after a Missourian of that name who he claimed had shown him kindness during his youth.[4]

In 1816, Hunter abandoned his Indian way of life and went to work with a group of fur traders. During the lulls in that business, he attended a school near Pearl River, Mississippi, and applied himself diligently to the study of the English language, writing, and arithmetic, in which he made much progress. In 1821 he crossed the Allegheny Mountains and went to New York, where he entered upon an entirely new life. He visited England in 1823–24 and was lionized by the fashionable world in London. Many philosophers, philanthropists, noblemen, and journalists found him an exciting man "whose travels over the world had been more exciting if possible, than those of Sinbad the Sailor."[5]

The most conspicuous characteristic of this unusual person was his demonstrated fondness for the untutored Indians. All his energies were expended in one direction—the promotion of civilization and knowledge among the scattered and decaying tribes of red men.[6] He first planned to extend the benefits of a civilized life to the Indians in the vicinity of the Quapaws in Arkansas. It is not known why he abandoned his original intention and went to the Cherokee village in Texas.[7]

Hunter was of middle height and inclined to stoutness. His face was expressive rather than handsome, with strong lines of a marked character. He was unusually quiet-mannered until he discussed his plans for the Indians. A contemporary, historian Henry Stuart Foote, observed:

Any discussion relative to the situation and character of the

[4] *Ibid.*
[5] *Ibid.*
[6] Foote, *Texas and the Texans*, I, 241.
[7] Winkler, "The Cherokee Indians in Texas," *loc. cit.*, 122.

Indians would rouse the level calm of his ordinary manner into a storm that agitated his entire soul. Grave, deliberate, and intelligent on every other subject, the moment that chord was touched, his enthusiasm and ardour overpowered the sluggishness of calculating investigation, and his imagination burned with the distant prospect of the civilization and happiness of the persecuted Indians . . . the long-cherished object of his philanthropic ambition.

Foote asked, "Can it be that this man was an impostor?" He answered the question emphatically: "I for one will not yet believe it."[8] He suggested that judgment of Hunter's character be suspended until more light could be shed upon the mystery. Then the public could condemn him with conviction or consecrate the memory of a martyr to philanthropy.

Foote was responding to journalistic attacks on Hunter's credibility. Among the journalists who believed that Hunter was an impostor was Frederick T. Gray, publisher of the *North American Review*. Gray sought to expose Hunter in a special article entitled "Indians of North America." He called Hunter one of the boldest impostors who had ever appeared in the literary world and his book a worthless fabrication beneath the dignity of criticism. He believed that Hunter's book had been compiled by a professional writer from earlier accounts and from Hunter's imagination.

Gray based his conclusions on letters he received from several persons who had knowledge of the Indians with whom Hunter claimed to have lived. One of them, General William Clark, a leader of the Lewis and Clark Expedition, had written that he would not hesitate to call Hunter an impostor and that many of the important events related in his book were outright falsehoods.

Baronet Vázquez, subagent for the Kansa tribe from 1796 to 1824, reported to Gray that during that time no white man of any age or description had lived among the Indians, nor did he

8 Foote, *Texas and the Texans*, I, 245–47.

believe that any white man had done so in the past thirty years.

Major P. Chouteau, who knew the Osages well, wrote Gray that he had been a trader and agent among members of that tribe since 1775 and that during those years no white boy had lived among them.

Probably the most convincing letter Gray received was from John Dunn, the man whose name Hunter had adopted. Dunn wrote that he had never known the man calling himself John Dunn Hunter. He had lived in the same region for the past twenty years, and during that time he had never heard of any person living there with the same name as his own.

Gray concluded: "I am therefore confident that the author alluded to is an impostor, and that the work issued under his name is a fiction . . . most probably the labor of an individual who had never seen the vicious tribes of Indians of whom he speaks." He added that it was the duty of his magazine to expose Hunter's character and the fraudulence of his work. It was important that, "if we cannot advance, we should not at least go backward in our knowledge of the history and character of the Indians."[9]

Hunter left London in 1824. Nothing is known of his travels until he arrived in Texas the following year.[10]

Soon after reaching Fields's village, which was still the main Cherokee headquarters north of Nacogdoches, Hunter became a leading influence among the Indians. He saw at once the tenuous hold they had on their land. He felt sure that, when it was convenient to do so, the Mexican government would dispense with any promises made to the Indians.[11] Without a legal title to their land the Cherokees could be driven from their homes and forced to return to the United States. Hunter persuaded Chief Fields to commission him to go to Mexico City and negotiate with the Mexican government on behalf of the Cherokees. Fields, believing that Hunter would know how to talk to the

[9] Frederick T. Gray, "Indians of North America," *North American Review,* n.s. Vol. XXII, No. 1 (1826), 94–107.

[10] Winkler, "The Cherokee Indians in Texas," *loc. cit.,* 122.

[11] Bancroft, *History of North Mexican States and Texas,* XVI, 103n.

authorities and that they would listen to him, granted Hunter permission to make the journey. He left the village in March, 1826, and returned in September of the same year.[12] His attempt at a settlement of title was fruitless.

Ellis P. Bean, Indian agent for the Mexican government, was in the Cherokee village when Hunter returned from Mexico. He attended the council meeting called soon afterward and heard both Fields and Hunter speak before the warriors. Bean wrote to Austin about the meeting and quoted Fields's speech:

> In my old days I traveled two thousand miles to the City of Mexico to get some lands to settle a poor orphan tribe of red people who looked to me for protection. I was promised lands for them after staying one year in Mexico and spending all I had. I then came to my people and waited two years, and then sent Mr. Hunter after selling my stock to provide him money for his expenses. When he got there he stated his mission to the government. They said they knew nothing of this Richard Fields and treated him with contempt. I am a red man and a man of honor and can't be imposed on this way. We will lift our tomahawks and fight for land with all those friendly tribes that wish land also. If I am beaten I will resign my fate, and if not I will hold lands by the force of my red warriors.

Bean saw the danger in the situation. He added the following postscript to his letter to Austin: "So my dear sir the only way to stop this is to come forward . . . and give them lands or the country will be entirely lost."[13]

Hunter addressed the council after Chief Fields. He painted a gloomy picture for the Indians. He told them that they could lose their homes and all they held dear in Texas. He warned them that, without a title, their lands could be taken away at any time unless they prepared to defend themselves "against the whole power of the Mexican Government by force of arms."[14]

The Cherokees were so stirred by the speeches that they were

[12] Starr, *History of the Cherokee Indians*, 193.
[13] Bennett Lay, *The Lives of Ellis P. Bean*, 114.
[14] Foote, *Texas and the Texans*, I, 248.

ready to declare war at once. They were already angry because immigrants from the United States had been coming into their territory. They would raid and plunder the intruders first. Hunter calmed them with quiet words. He told them that he also agreed to war but asked them to wait a few weeks. He would ride to Nacogdoches and talk with the *empresario*, Hayden Edwards, to learn how he felt about the Mexican government. The warriors agreed.[15]

Hunter went to Nacogdoches and had an interview with Hayden Edwards and his brother, Benjamin Edwards. After listening to a recital of their grievances against the Mexicans, he urged them to unite with the Indians, under his control and that of Chief Fields, in a war against the common enemy. After reaching a friendly understanding with them, he returned to the Cherokee village to obtain sanction for what he had done and to send a number of Indian warriors to Nacogdoches to aid the colonists.[16]

In the meantime, many settlers were becoming suspicious of Hunter. They knew that he was in league with the Cherokees and feared that trouble was brewing. James Kerr wrote Austin that he believed Hunter was a spy in league with the British. Kerr had been in Mexico the past winter when Hunter was there and had observed him in conference with General Arthur G. Wavell, who had a colonial grant to settle colonists in Mexico. Kerr believed that Hunter and Wavell planned to overthrow the Mexican government. Hunter would stir up the Indians on the frontier, and Wavell would land five hundred Englishmen at the mouth of the Brazos River. Once the Mexicans were defeated, the British would organize a government of their own. "Unlikely as such scheme would seem, when compared with reason and common sense," Kerr wrote, "yet we see some of its features demonstrated. Hunter has raised the hatchet and the blood hounds at his heels are ready to devour opposition."[17]

---

[15] *Ibid.*, 249.
[16] *Ibid.*, 249–50.
[17] *Austin Papers*, II, 1591.

By early fall there was much talk about the hostility of the Cherokees. On September 11, 1826, Austin wrote to the commander of Texas that the delay in measures concerning the peaceable tribes was a misfortune and that one hundred Cherokees were worth more as warriors than five hundred Comanches.[18]

Was Hunter an impostor? Was he a dedicated man, inspired by philanthropic motives? Did he really want to help the Cherokees, or had he formed a plot to overthrow the Mexican government and establish a new one in the wilds of Texas? Probably no one will ever know, but the role he played in Texas history would soon come to a tragic end.

[18] Starr, *History of the Cherokee Indians*, 193.

CHAPTER IV

The Fredonian Rebellion

In April, 1825, Hayden Edwards received a contract in Saltillo, Mexico, to settle eight hundred families in Texas.[1] His grant called for settlement of the region north of Nacogdoches to the margin of the reserved land on the coast. He was expected to settle the vacant lands in that area and to respect existing titles.[2] Edwards' territory included Nacogdoches, one of the oldest Spanish settlements in Texas. At that time it was dangerous country. On the east it adjoined a twilight zone, a refuge for the lawless, renegades and squatters where law was unknown. The people of Nacogdoches were a motley group composed of all races and classes, including rough American frontiersmen, Spanish and French Creoles, and substantial planters "accustomed to a gentler degree of civilization."[3] One historian wrote that the village was the haunt of gamblers and that counterfeiters operated openly.[4] Indians in varying stages of "civilization" frequented the town.[5] Most of these were, of course, Cherokees claiming a large area of East Texas, much of it included in the Edwards grant.[6]

[1] Eugene C. Barker, *Life of Stephen F. Austin, Founder of Texas, 1793–1836: A Chapter in the Westward Movement of the Anglo-American People*, 148–50. Hereafter cited as *Life of Austin*.

[2] Winkler, "The Cherokee Indians in Texas," *loc. cit.*, 176.

[3] Barker, *Life of Austin*, 148–50.

[4] Louis J. Wortham, *A History of Texas, from Wilderness to Commonwealth*, I, 225.

[5] Barker, *Life of Austin*, 148–50.

[6] Winkler, "The Cherokee Indians in Texas," *loc. cit.*, 116.

There had been ill will between the Anglo-Americans and the Mexicans from the time Nolan and Long made their expeditions into the country.[7] A Mexican alcalde ruled Nacogdoches, and preference was naturally given to the Mexican claimants of land titles.[8] Owing to the remote location of the town and the daily acts of lawlessness, it would have been remarkable if "anything approaching clean government [had been] administered there."[9]

Edwards had been in the country only a few weeks when he incurred the anger of many persons, especially the established settlers. He issued a proclamation October 25, 1825, ordering all persons residing within the territory, and all those holding claims to land in the territory, to present themselves to him and show their titles and documents in order that they could be approved or rejected. If they did not comply with the order their land would be sold. The order angered Chief Bowles as well as many old settlers of Nacogdoches. On December 15, Edwards issued a second proclamation calling for an election of militia officers which further angered authorities. Edwards also became involved in a heated election for alcalde in which his son-in-law, a man named Chaplin, defeated one Samuel Norris. This event climaxed the hard feelings between the newcomers and the old settlers. Edwards' opponents magnified his mistakes and misrepresented Chaplin's acts to the political chief. Chaplin was removed from office, and Norris was installed.[10]

---

[7] Philip Nolan led an expedition into Texas in 1800–1801, supposedly to capture wild horses. He fell under the suspicion of Spanish authorities because of an alleged conspiracy with Aaron Burr. Nolan and about half of his men were killed near present Waco, Texas. Nine were taken prisoner and sent to Mexico. *Texas Almanac, 1961–1962*, 326. Dr. James Long, of Mississippi, led an expedition into Texas in 1819 and captured Nacogdoches. His forces were later defeated. He led a second expedition into Texas from Point Bolivar in 1821, but was again defeated. He was imprisoned in Mexico and killed under mysterious circumstances. *Ibid.*, 327.

[8] James T. DeShields, *Border Wars of Texas, Being an Authentic and Popular Account, in Chronological Order, of the Long and Bitter Conflict Waged Between Savage Indian Tribes and the Pioneer Settlers of Texas* (ed. by Matt Bradley), 41. Hereafter cited as *Border Wars of Texas.*

[9] Wortham, *History of Texas*, I, 225.

[10] Winkler, "The Cherokee Indians in Texas," *loc. cit.*, 117, 135.

Edwards was charged with selling land and with failing to show his credentials to the alcalde. It was rumored that he had a large supply of arms in his home and that he had sold his colonial grant in New Orleans for $120,000 and planned to bring an army from the United States to fight the Mexicans.[11]

Austin, worried about Edwards' conduct, warned him by letter that if he continued his imprudent course he would be ruined and all the new settlements would suffer. Austin advised him to be more judicious in his remarks and observations. He had a difficult task to perform and was watched with a jealous eye. His most innocent expression could be misunderstood or willfully perverted. Austin told Edwards that nothing would injure him more than direct trouble and misunderstanding with the old Spanish settlers in his colony and urged him to use the utmost prudence in his dealings with them.[12]

With the accession of Norris to the alcalde's office, there commenced a period of tyranny which incensed the Anglo colonists. Many were evicted from their lands, which were turned over to the Mexicans who were favorites of Sepulveda, captain of the militia, and to Norris. James Gaines, Norris' brother-in-law, formed a band of regulators to force the colonists into submission. The Mexicans ruled as they wished.[13]

Terror reigned. Settlers were arrested at all hours, often dragged from their beds at night and taken before the alcalde. They were imprisoned and fined for acts and crimes they had not committed.[14]

Conditions continued to worsen. In the midst of the trouble Hayden Edwards had to go to the United States on business. He left his brother, Benjamin W. Edwards, in charge of colonial affairs.[15]

---

[11] Barker, *Life of Austin*, 160.
[12] Wortham, *History of Texas*, I, 219–20.
[13] Bancroft, *History of the North Mexican States and Texas*, II, 101.
[14] *Ibid.*, 102.
[15] Wortham, *History of Texas*, I, 236–38.

After continuous outrages suffered under the less than protective shield of Mexican law, the Americans decided to rid the country of the corrupt officials and their tyranny. Benjamin Edwards tried to restrain them from any hasty action. He wrote to B. J. Thompson on October 2, 1826:

> Let us wait and not prejudice our prospects by premature operations on our part. The government may yet act with faith and justice toward the Americans. . . . The eyes of the government are at this moment upon us all, and much may depend upon our present deportment. Gaines and Sepulveda have been represented to the proper authorities and in a little time an investigation must take place.[16]

The colonists waited six weeks for justice to be done. On November 22, thirty-six armed Americans, led by Martin Parmer, rode into Nacogdoches and arrested Norris and Captain Sepulveda. Unable to find James Gaines, they offered a reward of one hundred dollars for his capture, dead or alive. José Doste was appointed interim alcalde. Constituting themselves a court-martial, Parmer and his associates preferred charges against Norris and Sepulveda, tried them, and found them guilty. The two were released when they promised never to hold office again in the district.[17] Parmer and his men were acting in behalf of the outraged citizens and did not consider that their actions constituted a rebellion against the Mexican government.

Benjamin Edwards, fearing that his absent brother might lose his contract, wrote to Austin for advice. Austin told him to report the situation to Victor Blanco, governor of the province. Edwards did so, but his letter displeased the governor, who thought it lacked respect. He canceled Edwards' contract and ordered the brothers to leave the country.[18]

[16] Henderson Yoakum, *History of Texas, from Its First Settlement in 1685 to Its Annexation to the United States in 1846*, I, 244. Hereafter cited as *History of Texas*.

[17] Winkler, "The Cherokee Indians in Texas," *loc. cit.*, 136–37.

[18] Wortham, *History of Texas*, I, 236–38.

Hayden Edwards returned to Nacogdoches about the time his contract was annulled. He was incensed by the news. He had spent fifty thousand dollars on his colonial empire. If he was ejected from Texas, he would be ruined financially. He was determined to resist. He believed that he could enlist the aid of the colonists, the Cherokee Indians, their allies, and the United States in a revolt against Mexico.[19]

It must have seemed to Edwards an act of Providence that brought John Dunn Hunter and Chief Richard Fields to Nacogdoches at this crucial time. Hunter had persuaded Chief Fields to ally himself with the Edwards brothers and their followers. The fact that only a year had elapsed since Fields had threatened war against Edwards and his colonists is an indication of Hunter's influence over the chief. Moreover, conditions were different now. All were united in a common cause against a government they agreed was corrupt, base, and faithless. After a three-day powwow, a compact was signed by Fields and Hunter, acting for the Cherokees, Benjamin W. Edwards and Harmon B. Mayo signed as agents of the Committee of Independence. That unusual document read as follows:

Whereas, the Government of the Mexican United States, have, by repeated insults, treachery and oppression reduced the white and red emigrants from the United States of North America, now living in the Province of Texas, within the territory of said government, which they have been deluded by promises solemnly made, and most basely broken, to the dreadful alternative of either submitting their free-born necks to the yoke of the imbecile, unfaithful, and despotic government, miscalled a Republic, or of taking up arms in defense of their inalienable rights and asserting their independence; they . . . viz: the white emigrants now assembled in the town of Nacogdoches, around the independent standard on the one part, and the red emigrants who have espoused the same holy cause in order to prosecute more speedily and effectually the war of Independence, they have mutually

[19] *Ibid.*, 239–43.

undertaken to a successful issue and to bind themselves by the ligaments of reciprocal interests and obligations, have resolved to form a treaty of Union, League and Confederation.

For this illustrious object, Benjamin W. Edwards and Harmon B. Mayo, Agents of the Committee of Independence, and Richard Fields and John D. Hunter, the agents of the red people, being respectfully furnished with due powers, have agreed to the following articles:

1. The above named contracting parties bind themselves to a solemn union, league and confederation in peace and war to establish and defend their mutual independence of the Mexican United States.

2. The contracting parties guarantee mutually to the extent of their power, the integrity of their respective territories as now agreed upon and described, viz: the territory apportioned to the red people shall begin at the Sandy Spring where Bradley's road takes off from the road leading from Nacogdoches to the Plantation of Joseph Durst; from thence west by the compass, without regard to variation, to the Rio Grande; thence to the head of the Big Red River; thence north to the boundary of the United States of America; thence with the same line to the mouth of Sulphur Fork, thence in a right line to the beginning.

The territory apportioned to the white people shall comprehend all the residue of the Province of Texas, and of such other portions of the Mexican United States as the contracting parties, by their mutual efforts and resources, may render independent, provided the same shall not extend further west than the Rio Grande.

3. The contracting parties mutually guarantee the rights of *empresarios* to their premium lands only, and the rights of all other individuals, acquired under the Mexican Government and relating or appertaining to the above described territory, provided the said *empresarios* and individuals do not forfeit the same by an opposition to the independence of the said territories, or by withdrawing their aid and support to its accomplishment.

4. It is distinctly understood by the contracting parties that the territory apportioned to the red people is intended as well for the benefit of those tribes now settled in the territory apportioned to the white people as for those living in the former territory, and

that it is incumbent upon the contracting parties for the red people to offer the said tribes a participation in the same.

5. It is also mutually agreed by the contracting parties that every individual, red or white, who has made improvements within either of the respective allied territories and lives upon the same, shall have a fee simple of a section of land, including his improvements as well as the protection of the government in which he may reside.

6. The contracting parties mutually agree that all roads, navigable streams and all other channels of conveyance within each territory shall be open and free to the use of the inhabitants of the other.

7. The contracting parties mutually stipulate that they will direct all their resources to the prosecution of the Heaven-inspired cause which has given birth to this solemn union, league and confederation, firmly relying upon their united efforts, and the strong arm of Heaven for success.

Done in the town of Nacogdoches this the twenty-first of December, in the year of our Lord, one thousand eight hundred and twenty six. Richard Fields, John D. Hunter, B. W. Edwards, H. B. Mayo.

We, the Committee of Independence and the Committee of the Red People do ratify the above treaty, and do pledge ourselves to maintain it in good faith . . . Richard Fields, John D. Hunter, Ne-Ko-Lake, John Bags, Cuk-To-Keh, Martin Parmer, President, Hayden Edwards, W. B. Legon, John Sprowl, B. J. Thompson, Jos. A. Huber, B. W. Edwards, H. B. Mayo.[20]

Simply stated, the treaty gave the Indians all of the country west of the Bexar–Nacogdoches road from Red River to the Río Grande and gave the whites the rest of the province of Texas.[21]

Hayden Edwards had high hopes for the new Republic of Fredonia, the name the white settlers chose for their territory. On December 26, 1826, he wrote the colonists at Pecan Point telling them about the treaty made with the Cherokees, repre-

[20] Starr, *History of the Cherokee Indians*, 194–96.
[21] Barker, *Life of Austin*, 169.

senting twenty-three nations. Edwards requested that two delegates from every province be sent to Nacogdoches on the first Monday in February, 1827, when a declaration of independence would be drawn up and a government founded "upon the fundamental principles of the unalienable rights of man." He listed the grievances against the Mexican government. Lands had been granted and taken away at the will of a corrupt and prejudiced governor without any regard to the forms of justice or recourse to the judicial department of the government. Efforts had been made to take away the settlers' slaves. Innocent citizens had been bound hand and foot by brutal soldiers and sent into exile or locked in dungeons at the will of a petty tyrant—acts sanctioned by the governor. He concluded:

> Great God, can you any longer hesitate fellow citizens. . . . We have undertaken this glorious cause with determination to be free men or to perish under the flag of liberty. We are at least determined to live or to die like Americans and like the sons of free men.[22]

The Edwards brothers then visited the settlers between the Attoyac and Sabine and gathered a number of followers.[23] While riding back toward Nacogdoches several days later, they learned of a rumor that the enemy would be in Nacogdoches that night. The men delayed long enough to make a flag of red and white, inscribed with the words "Independence, Freedom, and Justice." Then they rode into Nacogdoches, seized the old stone fort, and proclaimed the Republic of Fredonia.[24] According to one historian, "Old Norther himself who so often swept over the plains of Texas stood aghast at the chilling exhibition."[25]

No enemy appeared, and the small band of patriots remained unmolested in the fort. During the next few days they levied supplies from the Mexican citizens, readied the fort for defense,

22 *Austin Papers*, II, 1544–45.
23 Foote, *Texas and the Texans*, I, 250.
24 Lay, *The Lives of Ellis P. Bean*, 114.
25 DeShields, *Border Wars of Texas*, 44.

strengthened their alliance with the Indians, and sought help from colonists in other parts of the state and from adjacent regions of the United States.[26]

Hayden Edwards sent letters to persons in the United States and to the Austin colonists, calling on all Anglo-Americans to "rally to the glorious Fredonian cause." His followers had planted the standard of liberty and independence, and, like their forefathers, they would support it or perish by it. "We are Americans and will die sooner than submit to slavery and oppression."[27]

Austin, a loyal and conscientious citizen of Mexico, was appalled by the rebellion. He would never have defied the Mexican laws at that time, and he found it hard to believe that Edwards had done so. Not for ten years would Austin himself take up arms against the Mexican government, and fight for independence.

Austin called the revolutionaries "a small party of infatuated madmen."[28] He told his colonists that it was their duty as Americans to defend the proud name of Texas from the infamy the Nacogdoches rebels would cast upon it if they were permitted to carry out their plans. Moreover, without government and law what security would the colonists have for their persons, their property, their characters, and all that they held dear?[29]

Austin did everything in his power to quell the Fredonian Rebellion. He persuaded Saucedo, the political chief, to offer a full pardon to the rebels, along with a promise to investigate their grievances, including Edwards' contract and the Cherokee claim for land, if they would give up their plan.[30] He wrote letters to Hunter and Fields and his fellow chiefs. To Hunter he wrote on January 4, 1827:

> Dear Sir, report has informed me of the interest you are taking in favor of the Cherokees. . . . Your object in uniting temporarily

[26] Winkler, "The Cherokee Indians in Texas," *loc. cit.*, 140.
[27] Wortham, *History of Texas*, I, 247.
[28] *Ibid.*, 254.
[29] *Ibid.*, 255.
[30] *Ibid.*, 260.

with the Nacogdoches insurrection is to procure land for the Cherokees from the Mexican Government. To suppose for one moment that your object is civil war and rebellion would be to suppose you destitute of that integrity and judgment which you have always manifested on all occasions so far as I have heard of you. . . . I know the Cherokees can get their lands if the legal steps are adopted, and if they take the wrong course they are lost. The ruin may not be immediate, but it will ultimately fall and overwhelm them and their friends. . . . Bring in the Cherokee chiefs to this place . . . and all will be right. If you are the man of talents I believe you to be and are actuated by the benevolent feelings toward the Cherokees which you profess, you will see that the favorable moment in the tide of their affairs has arrived and you will embrace it. Before the sword is drawn the government will yield a little to the Cherokees to keep it in its scabbard, but once drawn and stained with blood they will never yield one hair's breadth, and nothing short of extermination or expulsion of that nation will satisfy them. . . . As respects the Edwards they have been deceived. . . .This government has by letters offered a complete and full and unequivocal oblivion as to this occurrence at Nacogdoches. . . . Come therefore and bring the Cherokee chiefs and the Edwards brothers and see the chief of department and commandant of arms. . . . I pledge myself and this colony will sustain the pledge.[31]

Later that month, on January 23, Austin wrote to the Cherokee chiefs:

My brothers, I fear you have been deceived by bad men who wish to make use of you to fight their battles. They will ruin you and your people if you follow their council. The governor wrote to you and sent Judge Richard Ellis of Huntsville, Alabama, Mr. James Cummins from the Colorado and James Kerr from the Guadalupe to see you at Nacogdoches and tell you the truth, but I fear John D. Hunter has concealed the letter and the truth from you for he and Edwards would not suffer those men to talk with the Indians. . . . My brothers, why is it that you wish

[31] *Austin Papers*, II, 1565.

Chief Bowles of the Texas Cherokees, as conceived by William A. Berry. Courtesy John Jenkins, The Pemberton Press, Austin.

El Palacio de Gobierno, Saltillo, Mexico, where Chief Bowles and Chief Fields sought a title to the Cherokee lands in Texas. Courtesy William B. Alderman, Editor, *Texas Parade.*

William Augustus Bowles, who founded an Indian state in Florida called "Muscogee" and made himself the supreme ruler. He is not to be confused with Chief Bowles of the Texas Cherokees. Reprinted from R. S. Cotterill, *The Southern Indians: The Story of the Civilized Tribes Before Removal.*

"Dutch," the Western Cherokee chief who spent some time in Texas with Chief Bowles. Oil painting by George Catlin. Reprinted from Grace Steele Woodward, *The Cherokees*.

Mr. and Mrs. Hayden E. Edwards. Edwards organized the Republic of Fredonia and declared Texas independent of Mexico. Reprinted from Dudley G. Wooten (ed.), *A Comprehensive History of Texas, 1685 to 1899.*

The flag of the Republic of Fredonia once waved from this old stone fort in Nacogdoches, Texas. Reprinted from Dudley G. Wooten (ed.), *A Comprehensive History of Texas, 1685 to 1899.*

John H. Reagan. Reprinted from Dudley G. Wooten (ed.), *A Comprehensive History of Texas, 1685 to 1899.*

Ellis P. Bean, Indian agent. Reprinted from Homer S. Thrall, *A Pictorial History of Texas.*

to fight your old friends and brothers the Americans? God forbid that we should ever shed each others blood. . . . Let us be friends and live in peace and harmony. . . . The bad men who have been trying to mislead you have told you that we would all join them. . . . This is not true, not one of us will join them. . . . The Cherokees are a civilized and honorable people, and will you unite yourselves with wild savages to murder and plunder helpless women and children? . . . Edwards is deceiving you, he once threatened to take your land from you and would have done it if he could . . . leave him and come and see the governor and hear the truth.[32]

Both letters were delivered to Ellis, Cummins, and Kerr, instructing them to tell Edwards that Saucedo had offered a full pardon to all the insurrectionists if they would abandon their cause.[33] These overtures were useless. The Fredonians sent word that they would settle for nothing less than their "entire free, and unmolested independence from the Sabine to the Rio Grande."

When the men returned, however, they notified Austin that two Cherokee chiefs, Bowles and Big Mush, had refused to join Hunter and Fields in the rebellion.[34]

Since peace could not be restored, force would be necessary. On January 22, 1827, Austin addressed the colonists, telling them that the olive branch of peace had been insultingly returned. The Fredonians were exciting the Indians to murder and plunder. "To arms then, my friends and fellow-citizens, and hasten to the standard of our country," he urged.[35] On January 24 he called for mobilization. The first one hundred men would march toward Nacogdoches on January 26.

As they marched toward Nacogdoches, Austin and his colonists, along with the Mexican army under Mateo Ahumada, now a colonel, and José Antonio Saucedo, political chief in charge of

[32] *Ibid.*, II, 1593.
[33] Wortham, *History of Texas*, I, 269.
[34] *Austin Papers*, II, 1586–87.
[35] Starr, *History of the Cherokee Indians*, 196.

operations, numbered around four hundred men.[36] The Fredonians had numbered about two hundred followers at first, but their forces had decreased in the preceding two weeks. Quarrels had broken out among the insurgents, and political differences over the alcaldes had flamed anew. The large number of Indian warriors promised by Hunter and Fields did not show up. The Kickapoos in the area refused to be allied with the whites, whom they hated because of early injustices.[37] Not over thirty warriors had been willing to go to battle with Edwards, and half of them returned home when the Fredonians erupted in a drunken brawl.[38]

Bowles and Big Mush had refused to join the rebels for good reason. In December, Ellis Bean, Indian agent for the Mexican government, had left San Antonio with thirty-five Mexican soldiers to try to put down the rebellion. As he neared Nacogdoches, he was put to rout by Edwards and fifteen of his men carrying the Fredonian flag.[39] Bean camped north of Nacogdoches but immediately rode into the Indian country, urging the Cherokees not to join in the rebellion. Bean and his emissaries, Williams and Elliott,[40] promised the Indians land and fair treatment if they would remain loyal to the government.[41] Chief Bowles and Big Mush agreed to ally themselves with Bean.

In the meantime, the small band of Fredonians, fortified in the stone building in Nacogdoches, began to worry. They knew that their number was too small to fight the combined forces of Colonel Austin and Colonel Ahumada. Hunter and Fields were somewhere in the Cherokee country, trying to round up more recruits.[42] The Edwards brothers and their companions realized that their rebellion had failed and that there was but one alter-

---

[36] Wortham, *History of Texas*, I, 275.

[37] Yoakum, *History of Texas*, II, 248–50.

[38] Barker, *Life of Austin*, 169.

[39] Yoakum, *History of Texas*, II, 246.

[40] Williams and Elliott later received a league of land for this service. Wortham, *History of Texas*, I, 200.

[41] Yoakum, *History of Texas*, II, 248–50.

[42] Foote, *Texas and the Texans*, I, 279.

native left. They must flee across the Sabine into the United States before the colonists and soldiers reached Nacogdoches. Taking their beloved banner with them, they headed out the old San Antonio Road toward the Louisiana border, leaving their dreams of a free republic behind them. Not a shot had been fired in the short-lived Fredonian Rebellion. The fourpounder that Austin had brought up to attack the stone fort was never used.[43]

When calm had been restored in Nacogdoches, Austin wrote a friend that tranquillity had been restored, for which the entire country was grateful. The Mexican character stood higher than it ever had before.[44]

Yet all was not lost. As Emmet Starr wrote:

> The compact of the Fredonians was to them what the immortal document of 1776 was to the Americans during the gloomy days of the American Revolution. It was their divorcement from a weak, unstable and vacillating rule. It was the forerunner of the glory of San Jacinto.[45]

Because of the Fredonian flag that once waved so hopefully and defiantly above the old stone fort in Nacogdoches, that part of Texas can boast seven flags instead of the six that have waved over most of Texas during her history.

[43] Barker, *Life of Austin*, 174.
[44] *Austin Papers*, II, 1711.
[45] *History of the Cherokee Indians*, 196.

CHAPTER V

Chief Bowles Again Rules His People

J OHN Dunn Hunter and Chief Richard Fields paid with their lives for the part they played in the Fredonian Rebellion. According to one historian, Chief Bowles was hired to murder them, and did so brutally. Hunter was killed at a Cherokee village near the present town of Henderson, Texas.[1] According to Henry Stuart Foote, Hunter and Fields had been sent to the village for recruits. They tried without success to persuade the Indians to help the Fredonians. Hunter then decided to return to Nacogdoches alone to share the fate of the colonists. This decision angered the Indians. Two members of the tribe accompanied him. When he stopped to water his horse in a stream, he was shot in the shoulder by one of the Indians and fell into the water. As the Indian aimed at him again, Hunter begged him not to shoot, pleading that it was hard to die at the hands of friends. The second bullet killed him, and his body slowly sank in the blood-stained water.[2]

A few days later Chief Fields was killed in a camp across the Sabine where he had been hiding.[3]

Hunter's death was reported in the *Arkansas Gazette* of May 29, 1827. The article stated that not long before he had been

[1] Yoakum, *History of Texas*, II, 250; Emmet Starr, *Cherokees West, 1794–1839*, 153.

[2] Foote, *Texas and the Texans*, I, 280.

[3] *Lamar Papers*, III, 263.

murdered by two Indian assassins and that he had organized the Fredonian Rebellion because the Mexican government had made a promise to grant him a tract of land, which they refused to fulfill. Hunter then sought redress in a civil war and exerted his influence over the Cherokees to induce them to join his revolutionary plan. They gave him assurance of support but when the time came, refused to march.

It is uncertain whether Fields and Hunter were tried by the tribe,[4] or whether Chief Bowles took it upon himself to order their execution without the formality of a tribal ceremony. Nor is it known, if the trial was held, whether the defendants were present or tried *in absentia*.

The fact remains that both Hunter and Fields were killed, although some of the details are unknown. Thus, in a roundabout manner, they were the only casualties of the Fredonian Rebellion.

Ellis P. Bean, the Mexican Indian agent, might have conceived the plan to murder Hunter and Chief Fields, finding a willing accomplice in Bowles. Hayden Edwards wrote President Lamar that Bean was a man of notoriously bad character.[5] On the other hand, Woldert wrote that Bean was a loyal agent.[6] Whatever his character might have been, Bean must have realized that it would indeed be a feather in his cap if he could put down the rebellion. He first went to see Hunter and Fields, but he had little influence over them. They remained loyal to Edwards.[7] Then he went to see Bowles and Big Mush.[8] It was reported that he told Bowles that if he wanted land for his nation, he would not get it by joining Hunter; but if he killed Hunter and Fields, who were the leaders among the Indians, the war would end, and he, Bean, would pledge his life that the Mexican government

[4] Winfrey, "Chief Bowles of the Texas Cherokee," *loc. cit.*, 33.

[5] *Lamar Papers*, III, 263.

[6] "The Last of the Cherokees in Texas," *loc. cit.*, 200.

[7] Foote, *Texas and the Texans*, I, 280.

[8] Gatun-wa-li (Big Mush) means Bread Made into Little Balls. Woldert, "The Last of the Cherokees in Texas," *loc. cit.*, 199.

would give the Indians the land they wanted. Bowles was said to have agreed and sent one of his men in pursuit of Hunter and Fields.[9]

From the beginning, Chief Bowles had not been too enthusiastic about joining the Fredonians. He had not signed the treaty with Edwards and Mayo as had Fields, Hunter, and other chiefs. Fields had acted without the authority of his tribe, in opposition to Bowles and Big Mush.[10]

Perhaps Bowles was "on the fence," waiting to see how the tide would turn when Bean arrived. He was both cunning and wary and wanted to be on the winning side in any fight. He was willing to lead his warriors to battle but wanted to be sure they fought on the side that would give them their Texas lands. When Bean talked with Bowles and Big Mush and promised them the Cherokee domain and fair treatment if they would remain loyal to Mexico, the Cherokee chiefs joined Bean's forces.

Austin used his influence with the Mexican authorities to obtain pardon for the Fredonians who did not escape to the United States. Edwards later thanked Colonel Ahumada by letter for this generous act.[11]

After the death of Fields and Hunter, Bowles became war chief of the Texas Cherokees, and Big Mush succeeded Hunter as civil chief.[12]

Colonel Ahumada wrote Bustamente, captain general of the Internal Province, that Bowles and Mush, military and civil chiefs, had given orders to kill Hunter and Fields and that papers and a flag had been taken from the dead men and turned over to the Mexican authorities. Ahumada reported that Bowles and Big Mush had given every proof of their loyalty and love for the Mexican government, in return for which they hoped to receive a grant of land in the Mexican province of Texas for the

[9] *Lamar Papers*, III, 263.
[10] Barker, *Life of Austin*, 169.
[11] DeShields, *Border Wars of Texas*, 46.
[12] Winfrey, "Chief Bowles of the Texas Cherokee," *loc. cit.*, 33.

settlement of their tribe. He strongly recommended such a move to His Excellency:

> I beg you will take it into consideration in order that the reward may be granted them which they have earned by the valuable services they have rendered, and in view of the fact that they have offered to arrest and to deliver Edwards and other leaders of that faction in case they should cross this side of the Sabine River and visit their village.[13]

Bustamente made a favorable reply to Colonel Ahumada. He was relieved that "those perfidious demagogues Fields and Hunter" were dead. He would recommend that the Supreme Government give Bowles and Mush their land and believed the request would be granted.[14]

Bowles was praised by the Mexicans for the part he played in the Fredonian Rebellion.[15] In July of that summer (1827), he was made a lieutenant colonel in the Mexican Army in appreciation of his services. Bowles was highly pleased with that honor and rode proudly into Nacogdoches to place himself and his people at the disposal of the Mexican commander, Colonel José de las Piedras. Bowles told the Mexican official that he wanted to strengthen the friendship between his people and Mexico. In order to do so, he would place the education of two of his small sons under the care of the Mexican government.[16]

Bowles is supposed to have received a fine Mexican hat, the type worn by the Mexican officers at that time, when the title of lieutenant colonel was conferred upon him. He wore the hat with great pride and cherished it the rest of his life. He was later frequently addressed as "Colonel Bowles," which seemed to please him.

In 1830, General Terán, commandant general of the Eastern Interior States, determined to perfect the title to Cherokee land,

[13] Winkler, "The Cherokee Indians in Texas," *loc. cit.*, 150–51.
[14] *Ibid.*
[15] Winfrey, "Chief Bowles of the Texas Cherokee," *loc. cit.*, 33.
[16] Winkler, "The Cherokee Indians in Texas," *loc. cit.*, 153.

since the Act of 1830, which prohibited further emigration of Americans into Texas, had been passed. He wrote Governor Letona of Coahuila and Texas, asking him "with a view to the preservations of peace" to give the Cherokees the lands promised them.[17]

In March, 1832, Governor Letona ordered that the necessary documents for such title be furnished to Colonel José de las Piedras, commander of the military forces on the Nacogdoches frontier. Before that official could receive the documents, he was expelled from Nacogdoches by an uprising of Americans. Soon afterwards General Terán committed suicide and Governor Letona died of yellow fever. The death of those two officials and the dismissal of the third, all of whom were friendly toward, and interested in, the Cherokees, was a blow to Chief Bowles and his people. Vincente Filisola, who succeeded Terán, was himself an *empresario*, and part of his grant was in the Cherokee tract. Never again would Mexican officials work so diligently in the tribe's behalf.[18]

Despite these reverses, Chief Bowles did not give up hope and persevered in his fight for a title to the Cherokee lands. He went to Bexar in July, 1833, with a delegation of his warriors, taking a petition to the political chief. From there they went to Saltillo, capital of the Province of Coahuila and Texas. They were reassured that their claims would receive consideration, but since the greater part of their lands had passed from the Leftwich and Edwards grants into the hands of David G. Burnet and General Vincente Filisola, titles could not be granted until those contracts expired in December, 1835.[19]

Chief Bowles pointed out that his tribe had occupied and improved the lands many years before *empresario* grants had been made. He said that his tribe now numbered 150 families, about 800 people, and 200 of them were men. The Cherokees

---

[17] Starr, *History of the Cherokee Indians*, 197.
[18] *Ibid.*
[19] *Ibid.*, 197–98.

owned 3,000 head of cattle and as many hogs. They owned 600 head of horses.[20] The majority of his people knew how to read and write, and a school for young men was conducted in their village. The Cherokees cultivated their fields and wove their own cotton into cloth and made it into clothing.[21]

The governor was impressed with Bowles and his petition and could readily see that the Cherokees were an unusually civilized tribe of Indians, but he had no authority to grant a title. It was a question that the Supreme Government would have to decide. Bowles was promised that his people would not be disturbed until the government at Mexico City could settle the matter.[22]

In the meantime, the Cherokees were protected by the Mexican government, and their rights as citizens were upheld. In 1835, Ruiz José Francisco, commandant at Nacogdoches, wrote the alcalde that five or six families had established themselves in pasture lands of the Cherokees, doing damage and wounding cattle and deer. He ordered the alcalde to expel the families at once because peace was necessary.[23] He wrote again that Surveyor Stroud had dared to survey lands in the Cherokee strip which included the house of Big Mush, and he ordered that Stroud be summoned to appear and explain the matter.

It seems that Bean, the Indian agent who had promised that Bowles and his people would get their lands and fair treatment if they stayed out of the Fredonian Rebellion, advised Mexican officials not to give the Cherokees a title to their land. He said that they would bring in a large number of their people from the United States to settle on the land as soon as a title was received, and that those families were barbarous people and would keep American colonists from coming to that section of Texas. Bean thought it would be wiser to give the Cherokees

[20] Woldert, "The Last of the Cherokees in Texas," *loc. cit.,* 192.

[21] José María Sánchez, "A Trip to Texas in 1828" (trans. by Carlos E. Castaneda), *Southwestern Historical Quarterly,* Vol. XXIX, No. 4 (1926), 249–88.

[22] Thomas Maitland Marshall, *A History of the Western Boundary of the Louisiana Purchase, 1819–1841,* II, 135. Hereafter cited as *A History of the Western Boundary of the Louisiana Purchase.*

[23] Walter Prescott Webb *et al.* (eds.), *The Handbook of Texas,* II, 515.

land located next to the nations with whom the Mexicans were at war.[24]

Since the state had no authority to give the Indians a title to their lands, the government decided to carry out the suggestion of Indian Agent Bean. In May, 1835, the Congress of Coahuila and Texas passed the following measure:

> 1. In order to secure the peace and tranquility of the state, the governor is authorized to select out of the vacant lands of Texas that land which may appear most appropriate, for the location of the peaceable and civilized Indians which may have been introduced into Texas.
> 2. It shall establish with them a line of defense along the frontier to secure the state against the incursions of the barbarous tribes.[25]

This order did not settle the Cherokee question. The Cherokees had not sought the particular lands that the Mexican government had proposed to set aside for them; furthermore, the Indians did not want to live in that area. They wanted only the East Texas lands where they had lived beneath the tall pines for more than a decade, where their dead were buried, and where their children had been born. They refused to move to the frontier and lost the only chance they ever had for a legal title to Texas territory. The Mexican government never made another statement regarding Cherokee lands.[26]

On November 11, 1835, the Consultation of Texas was held in San Felipe, and the Provisional Government issued the following order:

> All land commissioners, *empresarios*, surveyors, or other persons in anywise concerned in the location of lands, are ordered forthwith to cease their operations during the agitated and unsettled state of the country and to continue to desist from further loca-

[24] Winkler, "The Cherokee Indians in Texas," *loc. cit.*, 161.
[25] Starr, *History of the Cherokee Indians*, 198.
[26] *Ibid.*

tions until the land office can be properly systematized by the proper authorities which hereafter may be established.[27]

Talk of revolution was on every tongue. The Anglo-Texans were rebelling against the Mexican government. War seemed inevitable. Probably Chief Bowles recalled the Fredonian Rebellion nine years earlier and wondered which side, if any, he would take in the coming struggle. He and General Sam Houston, who had been appointed commander in chief of the Texas Army, were old friends. Bowles had visited in Houston's home, and at one time they went to Galveston together.[28] Houston had always been friendly and loyal to the Cherokees. He had spent part of his boyhood among them in Tennessee, and Chief Ol-loo-te-ka had adopted him as his son and christened him Co-lon-neh, the Raven. In 1829, only a few years before, Chief John Jolly had made Houston a citizen of the Cherokee Nation in Arkansas.[29] For the time being, Bowles would put his trust in his white brother.

There were times when all was not peaceful among Chief Bowles and his own people. Renegade Indians sometimes broke the peace and attacked the white settlers. There was a natural enmity between the two races. The whites feared the Indians, and the Indians hated the whites for intruding upon their hunting grounds. In 1834, four of Chief Bowles's tribesmen ventured into the white settlement of Sarahville, at the Falls of the Brazos, near present-day Marlin, Texas. One of them entered a cabin and stabbed the homesteader. Before another cabin could be attacked, several colonists appeared and a skirmish took place. Two of the Indians were killed, and a settler was wounded.

Sterling C. Robertson, colonizer of that area of Texas, wrote Chief Bowles about the attack, saying that the Indians had started the trouble. He wrote that his people had always been

---

[27] Winkler, "The Cherokee Indians in Texas," *loc. cit.*, 164.

[28] Harriett Smithers (ed.), *Journals of the Fourth Congress of the Republic of Texas, 1839–1840*, II, 103. Hereafter cited as *Journal of Fourth Congress*.

[29] Marquis James, *The Raven: A Biography of Sam Houston*, 127. Hereafter cited as *The Raven*.

kind to the Cherokees, had fed them and treated them like brothers. "I hope the fray will not make any difference between us and the Cherokees," he concluded.

Several months later, Robertson received the following letter, written on March 10, 1835, from Henry Rueg, political chief of the Department of Nacogdoches:

> On the 26th of febry last I held a talk with Col. Bowls, and some other chiefs of the Cheroqui nation, settled near this place, when said Bowls showed me a letter from you which I had interpreted to him, and after hearing its content he said he was satisfied, that it is the same statement made to him by the Indians. . . . Col. Bowls requested me very particularly to answer your letter for him, and tell you that he and his nation are perfectly satisfied with the course you have pursued with regard to the two indians . . . that he does not blame you nor your people in the least, but said you were justified in having done what you dit [did], he has enjoined upon all his young men to behave themselves better, and he hopes that you will take them by the hand as brothers should any of them come among you in the course of their hunting expedition and begs you to forget the past occur[r]ences and burry [sic] it in oblivion, as if it had never happened, which I communicate to you for the satisfaction of yourself and the citizen[s] of your part of the country.[30]

This letter showed Chief Bowles's sincere desire to keep the peace and to live in harmony with his white neighbors.

[30] Sterling C. Robertson Papers, Doctor Malcolm McLean, Texas Christian University, Fort Worth, Texas.

CHAPTER VI

The Cherokees Negotiate a Treaty

IT was November, 1835. For the third time, Texas delegates gathered in the small river town of San Felipe de Austin, colonial headquarters on the Brazos River, to talk over their problems and see what could be done about them. They had met there before, in 1832 and 1833.[1] Austin had addressed the people on September 19, 1835, urging every district to send members to the meeting, called the General Consultation of Texas, with full powers to do whatever was necessary for the good of the colony.[2] The delegates were high-strung and nervous. A seemingly inevitable war with Mexico and the Indian troubles were dark clouds upon the horizon. All the delegates realized the necessity of keeping the peace with the red men at that crucial time.

Dr. Branch T. Archer, of Brazoria, who had served as speaker of the Virginia House of Delegates before going to Texas, was elected president of the General Consultation, which began its business on November 3. He stressed the need to establish a provisional government with legislative and executive powers and the importance of making peace with the Indians. He said that several warlike, as well as peaceful, tribes claimed portions of the country and that settlers had located inside those lands, acts which had caused much dissatisfaction among the tribes. He

---

[1] *Texas Almanac, 1961–1962*, 329.
[2] Starr, *History of the Cherokee Indians*, 198.

"deemed it expedient to make some equitable arrangement of the matter that will prove satisfactory to them."[3]

A provisional government was established on November 11, and officers were elected on November 12. Henry Smith was elected governor and James W. Robinson, lieutenant governor. One of the primary duties of the newly organized government, as stressed by Archer, was to treat with the Indians regarding their land titles and to secure their friendship if possible. At that time the Cherokees living in East Texas were considered primarily farmers and stock raisers. They were not looked upon as "savage" or hunter Indians but rather as members of a civilized nation. What was perhaps more important, they had several hundred warriors who were expert with the rifle.[4]

On November 13 a "Solemn Declaration" was unanimously adopted by the fifty-four members of the consultation. It read as follows:

Be it solemnly decreed, that we, the chosen delegates of the Consultation of the people of all Texas, in general convention assembled, solemnly declare that the Cherokee Indians, and their associate bands, twelve tribes in number, agreeably to their last general council in Texas, have derived their just claims to lands included within the bounds hereinafter mentioned from the Government of Mexico, from whom we have also derived our rights to the soil by grant and occupancy.

We solemnly declare that the boundaries of the claims of the said Indians to the land is as follows, to-wit: lying north of the San Antonio road and the Neches, and west of the Angelina and Sabine Rivers. We solemnly declare that the Government and General Council, immediately on its organization shall appoint commissioners to treat with the said Indians to establish the definite boundaries of their territory, and secure their confidence and friendship.

We solemnly declare that we will guarantee to them the peaceful enjoyment of their rights to the lands, as we do our own; we

[3] *Ibid.*
[4] *Ibid.*, 199.

solemnly declare that all grants, surveys, and locations of lands, hereinbefore mentioned, made after the settlements of said Indians, are, and of right ought to be, utterly null and void, and that the commissioners issuing the same, be and are hereby ordered, immediately to recall and cancel the same, as having been made upon lands already appropriated by the Mexican Government.

We solemnly declare that it is our sincere desire that the Cherokee Indians and their associate bands, should remain our friends in peace and war, and if they do so, we pledge the public faith for the support of the foregoing declarations.

We solemnly declare that they are entitled to our commiseration and protection, as the just owners of the soil, as an unfortunate race of people, that we wish to hold as friends, and treat with justice. Deeply and solemnly impressed with these sentiments as a mark of sincerity, your committee would respectfully recommend the adoption of the following resolution . . . done in convention at San Felipe de Austin, this 13th day of November, A. D. 1835.[5]

Many notable signatures appear on that historic document, including those of Sam Houston, John A. Wharton, Lorenzo de Zavala, A. Horton, Henry Millard, Jesse Grimes, and Henry Smith. There is no reason to doubt that they signed in good faith, believing that such a treaty was just and would unite the settlers and Indians in a bond of friendship and understanding. Emmet Starr wrote that "language could not be made plainer or more obligatory than was this guarantee to the Indians."[6]

Houston was delighted that the "Solemn Declaration" had been unanimously adopted. Probably it would never have become a reality had he not put his weight behind it. Houston, the newly elected commander in chief of the Texas Army was a strong and impelling personality, and there is no doubt that he did much eloquent electioneering among his friends to help pass the proposal. He was an old friend of the Cherokee tribe and

---

[5] *Journal of the Consultation Held at San Felipe de Austin, October 16, 1835,* Barker Texas History Library, Austin, 51.

[6] *History of the Cherokee Indians,* 200–201.

wanted them to know of his loyalty.[7] After the document had been signed, Houston wrote his friend Chief Bowles on November 22, 1835:

> All that I promised . . . has been done and your land is secured to you. So soon as it is possible you will find commissioners sent to you to hold a treaty and fix your lines, that no bad men will go inside them without leave. I expect I will be sent to you and I will then take you the great paper that was signed by all the council . . . it will make you happy and all your people contented as long as you live.[8]

In his first speech after his election, Governor Smith urged delegates to second the measure of the consultation regarding the Cherokee question and "never [to] desist until the objects contemplated by that body be carried into effect."[9]

A few days later the governor advised the governing council to appoint a committee to implement the Indian treaty, based on the "Solemn Declaration" that had been signed at the convention. Observing that the United States government often sent its most distinguished military officers to perform such duties because the Indians respected such authorities, he thought that it would be wise to send General Houston of the army and Colonel John Forbes of Nacogdoches, whom he had commissioned one of his aides.[10]

A few days later General Houston, Colonel John Forbes, and John Cameron were appointed commissioners to confer with the Cherokees as soon as possible about the treaty. Houston and Forbes arrived in Bowles's village in mid-February (Cameron was unable to go with them). The commissioners found the Indians restless and suspicious of the whites. It took Houston several days to calm them down. He and Forbes slept in a

[7] Mooney, *Myths of the Cherokee*, Pt. I, 144.
[8] Winfrey, "Chief Bowles of the Texas Cherokee," *loc. cit.*, 35.
[9] Marshall, *A History of the Western Boundary of the Louisiana Purchase*, II, 138.
[10] Woldert, "The Last of the Cherokees in Texas," *loc. cit.*, 183.

house in the village and held daily conferences with the old chief and his warriors. Houston pledged his honor and authority as commander in chief of the Texas Army to support the treaty, which, he assured Bowles, would bring peace to the Cherokee people.[11]

The treaty, the first negotiated by the Provisional Government of Texas,[12] was signed in Bowles's village on February 23, 1836. Houston and Forbes signed for the government, and Colonel Bowles, Big Mush, Samuel Benge, Osoota, Corn Tassle, The Egg, John Bowles (the chief's son), and Tenuta signed for the Cherokees, Shawnees, Delawares, Kickapoos, Quapaws, Buloies, Iowanes, Alabamas, Coushattas, Caddoes of Neches, Tamocuttakes, and Untanguous.[13] The treaty contained thirteen articles.[14] The first declared that there should be a firm and lasting peace forever between both parties and that friendly intercourse should be pursued.

The second article stated that the tribes should possess the following lands:

> Beginning on the west at the point where the said road crosses the River Angelina, and running up said river, until it reaches the mouth of the first large creek below the great Shawnee village emptying into the said river from the northeast, thence running with said creek to its main source and from thence a due north line to the Sabine River and with said river west; then starting where the San Antonio road crosses the Angelina River and with said road to the point where it crosses the Neches River and thence running up the east side of said river in a northwest direction.[15]

The territory thus set aside was approximately fifty miles long and thirty miles wide and comprised present-day Smith and

[11] M. K. Wisehart, *Sam Houston, American Giant*, 163–64.
[12] R. Earl McClendon, "The First Treaty of the Republic of Texas," *Southwestern Historical Quarterly*, Vol. LII, No. 2 (1948–49), 32.
[13] Woldert, "The Last of the Cherokees in Texas," *loc. cit.*, 182.
[14] Dorman H. Winfrey *et al.* (eds.), *Texas Indian Papers, 1844–1845*, II, 14.
[15] *Ibid.*

Cherokee counties, and parts of Van Zandt, Rusk, and Gregg counties.[16]

Article Three of the treaty stipulated that "all lands granted or settled in good faith previous to the settlement of the Cherokees, within the before described bounds, are not conveyed by this treaty, but excepted from its operation." The Article further specified that any such previous settlers who may have moved from the area would be treated as intruders if they attempted to return. A subsequent article forbade selling any part of the lands involved, except to the Texas government. The Indians could not sell or lease land to any person who was not a member of their tribe, nor could any citizen of Texas buy or lease land from the Indians. The government of Texas would regulate trade and intercourse, but no taxes would be levied on the Indians. The Indians were granted the right to govern themselves within their own territory, as long as their laws were not contrary to those of Texas. It was agreed that one or more Indian agencies would be established and that at least one agent would reside within the Cherokee village to see that no injustice was done to the Indians.[17]

The question whether the Cherokees would support a military campaign against the Mexican government was not discussed in the treaty. The neutrality of the tribe was the goal sought by the Texans. (In this they were successful.) One historian has written that most of the battles for Texas' independence were fought in the Gulf Coast and southern areas of Texas. From those battles, of course, the Indians were too far removed to provide any material assistance.[18] However, it would prove impossible to give the Cherokees a deed to the land set aside in the treaty because the land office would be closed and remain so during the revolution.[19]

[16] Woldert, "The Last of the Cherokees in Texas," *loc. cit.*, 182–83.

[17] Winfrey, *Texas Indian Papers*, I, 14–16.

[18] Burton, "The Cherokee War," *loc. cit.*

[19] Anna Muckleroy, "The Indian Policy of the Republic of Texas," *Southwestern Historical Quarterly*, Vol. XXV, No. 4 (1922), 258.

After signing the treaty with Bowles, General Houston reportedly presented Chief Bowles with a sword, a silk vest, and a sash,[20] as well as, according to some historians, a military hat. A contemporary of Bowles said when he later saw the chief on the battlefield, Bowles wore hat, vest, sash, and carried the sword which had been given to him by General Houston.[21]

After the treaty was signed, there was a brief period of peace and good will. Texans breathed easier. Bowles and his people believed their land secure, and he kept the faith with his brother Houston. He had the great paper, decorated with seal and ribbons, which the commander in chief of the Texas Army had given him.[22] That paper, which made the Cherokee lands secure, Bowles guarded as a sacred trust. Houston's name was upon it. Bowles's mark was upon it. They were men of honor. All was well. It may have been during those few short months of peace and good will that old Chief Bowles at times fraternized with his white friends and went as far as to invite them to his village and to his lodge, where he served them venison stew.[23]

Mrs. Samuel Maverick recalled an occasion when Chief Bowles and perhaps a dozen members of his tribe camped at Spring Hill, near the Maverick home, on a return trip from the town of Houston. That night, while the Texans were dancing, Chief Bowles, with feathers in his hair and wearing a breechcloth, anklets, moccasins, and a long white linen shirt given to him by Houston, joined the party. Bowles told them that he had given Houston his daughter for his wife and had made Houston a "big chief." Since Bowles was the leader of the entire confederation of Texas Indian tribes, "an alliance with his daughter would have been in the political tradition of Houston's marriages."[24] Bowles told the Mavericks that Houston was no

[20] Woldert, "The Last of the Cherokees in Texas," *loc. cit.*, 185.

[21] Reagan, *Memoirs*, 29–36.

[22] Sam Houston, *The Writings of Sam Houston* (ed. by Amelia W. Williams and Eugene C. Barker), II, 131. Hereafter cited as *Writings*.

[23] Hattie Joplin Roach, *A History of Cherokee County*, 13.

[24] Jack Gregory and Rennard Strickland, *Sam Houston with the Cherokees, 1829–1833*, 84.

longer a Cherokee but "the great father" of the white men. When Bowles boasted that the pretty ladies in Houston danced with him, kissed him, and gave him rings, the Maverick guests begged to be excused, and the Cherokee chief was said to have stalked out with contempt.[25]

General Houston was too busy during those hectic months preceding the revolution to spend much time with his Cherokee friends, but there is no doubt that he missed those associations. He had a warmth and friendship for Chief Bowles and his people that many Texans could not understand, but he had lived with the Cherokees and knew their sincerity and loyalty. On those nights when Houston could join his friends, the campfires of Indians from various tribes could be seen burning on his lawn, where they spent the night after visiting with him. It was said that the general often sat with the Indians on a bearskin beside the campfire, "praising the flavor of the dog meat."[26]

[25] Mary Rowena Maverick Green (ed.), *Samuel Maverick, Texan: 1803–1870*, 70.
[26] James, *The Raven*, 292.

CHAPTER VII

"Null and Void"

AFTER his return from Bowles's village in the spring of 1836, Houston no doubt gave his copy of the Cherokee treaty to Governor Smith. On March 11, Smith surrendered his official documents to the convention at Washington-on-the-Brazos, where independence had been declared. The interim government was created on March 16, 1836. David G. Burnet was chosen president by the delegates. There seems to be no record that the interim government ratified the treaty,[1] an understandable oversight—the government was too harassed and too busy—and mostly on the move.

As busy as Houston was, trying to outmaneuver the Mexican hordes of Santa Anna's army, he wrote to his old friend Bowles from Gonzales on April 13, just eight days before the Battle of San Jacinto:

> I am busy and will only say how da do to you. You will get your land as it was promised in our treaty, and you and all my red brothers may rest satisfied that I will always hold you by the hand and look at you as brothers, and treat you as such. . . . Our army are all well and in good spirits. . . . Give my best compliments to my sister and tell her that I have not wore out the moccasins she made me.[2]

[1] Muckleroy, "Indian Policy," *loc. cit.*, Vol. XXV, 258.
[2] *Lamar Papers*, II, 69.

Frank X. Tolbert wrote in *The Day of San Jacinto* that the Indian sister Houston referred to was Mary Bowles, the chief's granddaughter. Mary often gave Houston gifts of her handiwork. On one occasion she gave him a vial of spirits made by distilling liquid from the shavings of deer horns. Houston believed that this was a good remedy for colds and carried the vial in his breast pocket, sniffing it frequently. Tolbert wrote that Houston developed a nervous habit of putting the vial to his nose, which may later have caused a hostile subordinate to accuse the general of eating opium.[3]

The revolutionary days of that unforgettable spring of 1836 dragged by, full of uncertainty and dread for every citizen of Texas. No one could predict what would happen next. The mere mention of the Alamo and Goliad filled every heart with fear and despair. Would the Mexican army under Santa Anna defeat the Texans? Would the Cherokees keep the treaty, or would their warriors, excellent marksmen, and their allied tribes join the Mexicans against the whites? If they did, the colonists had little chance for victory. They could not fight a combined force of Mexicans and Indians.

David Burnet, president of the interim government, hoped to keep the Indians pacified and realized that their neutrality was imperative. At one time he sent M. B. Menard to visit the Indians with $2,000 worth of presents and instructions that Menard was not to make any specific treaty relating to boundaries that might compromise "interests of actual settlers." Menard was to tell the Indians that the government was too busy at the present time to make positive treaties, but that "ample justice would be rendered them as soon as foreign relations could be adjusted on a peaceable footing . . . and lands adequate to their wants would be fully granted for their exclusive use."[4]

The first election in the new Republic of Texas was held in

[3] *The Day of San Jacinto*, 48–49.
[4] Muckleroy, "Indian Policy," *loc. cit.*, Vol. XXVI, 3–4.

September, 1836.[5] Sam Houston was elected president. In his inaugural address given on October 22, 1836, he said:

> A subject of no small importance is the situation of an extensive frontier, bordered by Indians, and open to their depredations. Treaties of peace and amity, and the maintenance of good faith with the Indians, present themselves to my mind as the most grounds on which to obtain their friendship. Let us abstain on our part from aggressions, establish commerce with the different tribes, supply their useful and necessary wants, maintain even-handed justice with them, and natural reason will teach them the utility of our friendship.[6]

The Indian treaty that Houston and Forbes had signed with the Cherokees was sent to the Texas senate in December, 1836, when Houston made the following speech in its behalf:

> . . . you will find upon examining this treaty that it is just and equitable and perhaps the best which could be made at the present time. It only secures to the said Indians usufructuary right to the country included within the boundary described in the treaty and does not part with the right of the soil, which is in this government; neither are the rights of any citizen of the Republic impaired by the views of the treaty but are all carefully secured by the third article of the same.
>
> In considering this treaty you will doubtless bear in mind the very great necessity of conciliating the different tribes of Indians who inhabit portions of country almost in the center of our settle-ments as well as those who extend along our frontier. This becomes the more judicious at present when we are at war with Mexico, the authorities of which have been laboring to engage the different tribes to war against us; and it has been confidentially stated that these Indians are among the number who have already engaged to join the Mexican army against us in the event of a second invasion, they being induced doubtless by promises of land and country; and should you ratify and confirm this treaty it doubt-

[5] *Texas Almanac, 1961–1962,* 331.
[6] McClendon, "First Treaty," *loc. cit.,* 41.

less would tend to secure their permanent friendship, a thing at this time much to be desired.[7]

No action on the treaty was taken at that time, but a committee headed by I. W. Burton was appointed to study the terms of the treaty.

By that time most Texans did not want the treaty ratified. They believed the rumor that Bowles had assembled his warriors on the San Antonio Road east of the Neches River and was planning to attack the Texans if they should be defeated by Santa Anna.[8] Many settlers believed that the Indians were enemies at heart and would turn on the whites when the opportunity came.[9] In other words, the Cherokees were "a red island in a white sea," and it was considered inevitable that the Anglo-Americans would submerge that island.[10]

During the spring of 1837 a party of Mexicans was said to have visited the frontier Indians. They had reportedly urged the Indians to make war against the whites and had promised to give them arms and ammunitions, all booty taken, and the whites' lands, if the Americans were driven out.[11]

Naturally the Indians were restless and not entirely trustful of the settlers. By now the Battle of San Jacinto had been fought and the Mexican army defeated, but the Cherokee treaty had not yet been ratified. It was to be expected that at least a few of the Indians listened to the grandiose promises of the Mexican agents.

President Houston heard about the Mexican overtures and, to show his loyalty to Bowles, offered him the commission of

[7] Ernest William Winkler (ed.), *Secret Journals of the Senate, Republic of Texas, 1836–1845*, 35–36.

[8] John H. Reagan, "Expulsion of the Cherokees from East Texas," *Quarterly of the Texas State Historical Association*, Vol. I (1897–98), 38–46. Hereafter cited as "Expulsion of the Cherokees."

[9] Brown, *History of Texas from 1685 to 1892*, II, 154.

[10] Walter Prescott Webb, *The Texas Rangers: A Century of Frontier Defense.* Hereafter cited as *The Texas Rangers*.

[11] A. K. Christian, "Mirabeau Buonaparte Lamar," *Southwestern Historical Quarterly*, Vol. XXIV, No. 1 (July, 1920–April, 1921), 45.

brigadier general in the Texas Army at two thousand dollars a year if he served actively or one thousand dollars a year if he did nothing. He also offered to take Bowles's warriors into the army at ninety-six dollars a head. Such an offer, if it had been accepted would have cost the government of Texas more money than the upkeep of a well-disciplined frontier army.[12]

Houston had been accused of showing greater leniency toward the Indians than he would have shown to his own countrymen.[13] Perhaps the offer to Bowles was the basis for this accusation.

The president hoped until the last that the senate would ratify the treaty, and despite his many duties, he kept in touch with his Indian friends. During the summer of 1837 he sent Chief Bowles on a mission to the prairie tribes to see whether they could be persuaded to sign a peace treaty with the whites. Bowles was away for several weeks. He found all the Indians willing to sign such a treaty except for the main tribe of Comanches. The reluctant Comanches were a numerous group living in a village several miles long on the Red River. They would not listen to peace talks and threatened to kill Bowles. A friendly chief helped the Cherokee leader escape. William Goyens visited Bowles's village after the chief had returned home and made a written report to President Houston. According to Goyens, Bowles was absolutely loyal to Houston and was worried because a rumor had been circulated that he was forming a league with the Indians to fight the Texans and was afraid Houston would believe it. "The confidence he has in you is unabated; he looks to you for everything," Goyens reported. He concluded his letter by saying that the Cherokee people were so happy to have Bowles back after his narrow escape with the Comanches that they celebrated for several days.[14]

At the October, 1837, session of congress, nearly ten months after the treaty had first been submitted to the senate, the com-

---

[12] Smithers, *Journal of Fourth Congress*, II, 103.

[13] Houston, *Writings*, II, 323–47.

[14] *Telegraph and Texas Register* (Houston), June 13, 1837; Blake Collection, *loc. cit.*, L, 125–27.

mittee made its report: the Cherokee treaty would be detrimental to the Republic of Texas and a violation of the legal rights of many citizens. The consensus of the committee was that the early promises made to the Indians by the Mexicans were false because the territory granted to the Indians formed a part of the Burnet colonization grant. The region already contained many completed titles, while others were in process of fulfillment. The committee believed that the Mexican government had never given or made any binding promises or grants to the Cherokees, or they would not have granted the land to Burnet.[15] As a result of the report the senate refused to ratify the treaty when it came up for discussion in December, 1837. On December 26 it was declared "null and void."[16]

Did the committee reject the treaty because they did not trust Bowles and felt he was not loyal to the Texans? He had not fought with them in the revolution against Santa Anna.[17] Houston wrote that, by the terms of the treaty, the Cherokees were not bound to take up arms for defense but were to remain neutral.[18] Houston maintained that that promise alone had meant much to the Texans. They had been greatly outnumbered by the Mexicans, and the prospects of a combined Mexican-Indian army had been too hazardous and hopeless to conjecture. Can it have been that the *empresarios*, one of whom had served as interim president, used their influence to see that the treaty was rejected because they wanted the Cherokee lands for their own exploitation?

One can imagine Houston's disappointment and distress when the senate refused to ratify the Cherokee treaty. He had given Bowles his word that the treaty would be honored and the boundary lines adhered to. He felt strongly about the breaking of the treaty and told congress on one occasion that if it had not been

---

[15] Winfrey, *et al.*, *Texas Indian Papers*, I, 26–27; Winkler, *Secret Journals of the Senate, Republic of Texas, 1836–1845*, 35–36.

[16] Muckleroy, "Indian Policy," *loc. cit.*, Vol. XXVI, 17–18.

[17] Winkler, *Secret Journals of the Senate, Republic of Texas, 1836–1845*, 36.

[18] Houston, *Writings*, II, 319.

signed the Cherokees would have taken up the tomahawk in defense of their rights and that, in addition to the Mexicans, the Texans would have had "a powerful Indian foe to contend with." Through fidelity to the whites, he said, the Indians had not taken up arms at a time when the settlers could easily have been driven from the country, that the Cherokees had been true to the Texans in their hour of danger.[19]

Houston, understandably disturbed by the Texans' unwilling-ness to ratify the treaty he had signed with Chief Bowles, let the congress know his feelings. A sacred pledge made in the time of peril had been disregarded, he said, adding that the Texans wanted to make "a Poland of the little patrimony of the Indians by parcelling it out among the crowned heads, of which they bore a conspicuous place." He recalled his sympathy for Bowles and his fellow leaders as they had stood in the halls of congress in Columbia, hoping that their treaty would be ratified. Many of the Indians had understood English well enough to know that the heated discussion taking place was not in their favor, and it was "enough to drive them mad." Houston was sure that the Chero-kees had returned to their village with a vengeful attitude toward the settlers and planning war against them.[20]

In the summer of 1838, Houston appointed Alexander Horton to lay out the boundary line between Cherokee and white terri-tory. He told Horton that, if the line had not been demarked by October 20, force would be employed to see that it was.[21] He had promised Bowles that the line would be laid out, and he intended to keep his promise.[22]

Houston also wrote General Thomas Jefferson Rusk, com-mander of the Texas militia, ordering him to have the line laid out according to the treaty of 1836:

It will do more to conciliate the Indians and give protection to

[19] *Ibid.*, 346.
[20] *Ibid.*, I, 323–47.
[21] McClendon, "First Treaty," *loc. cit.*, 43.
[22] Christian, "Mirabeau Buonaparte Lamar," *loc. cit.*, Vol. XXIV, 71.

the eastern section of Texas, than ten thousand men in the field would produce. If it is not immediately done, all future calamities must be attributed to its omission. I am satisfied if it is not done there will be another "Run-Away Scrape" and Eastern Texas will be desolated. . . . If it is not done an Indian war may ensue which may cost more blood and treasure than ought to purchase twenty such Indian countries, emigration will be stopped and the misfortunes resulting will not be retrieved in ten years.[23]

Feeling was high about the demarcation of the boundary line, and quarrels arose. Land speculators claiming disputed regions were angry, as were citizens (and soldiers) trying to locate land certificates in the rich territory. Many other Texans were afraid to have the Indians living in their midst.

When Chief Bowles learned of the quarrels, he wrote Horton that he had twenty-five men ready to stand guard while the boundary line was marked off and expressed his regrets that the whites objected to it. He assured Horton that the Indians wanted to do right and hoped that the white people wanted to do the same. He said he had ordered his men to take no part in the quarrels and disputes among the whites. Their duty was to guard Horton and the Indians' property. "I hope you will be particular with us in consequence of us not understanding your tongue and also we will pay that respect to you," he wrote.[24]

When disturbances continued over the boundary line, Bowles and his people became frightened. The chief wrote Houston that his people "from the biggest to the least have a little dread on their minds."[25] Houston replied that the conflict had begun before the surveyor had had time to mark the line but assured Bowles that the work would continue:

I wish it well done, that it may stand always. And that our children's children may live by it in peace and that our words may never be forgotten while time shall last. . . . I have given an order

[23] Houston, *Writings*, II, 289.
[24] *Lamar Papers*, II, 271.
[25] *Ibid.*, 200.

that no families or children of Indians shall be disturbed or have trouble, but they shall be protected and property not be troubled.[26]

On August 12, 1838, Houston wrote George May to tell Big Mush that the line would be done before the leaves fall "or I will give them my life or my land for I will not tell them a lie."[27]

On November 10, 1838, Horton wrote Houston that, after a tiresome and disagreeable route, he had succeeded in running the line between the whites and the Cherokees, despite persons in the neighborhood of Nacogdoches who were determined to involve the country in an Indian war. He reported that he had left Nacogdoches on October 11 for the frontier but that, before he reached it, a battle had been fought between Rusk and the Indians, which made his undertaking dangerous. On discovering the determination of some to drive off the Cherokees, "right or wrong, for individual speculation or self-agrandisement, regardless of blood of innocent women and children," he was nevertheless determined to execute his orders or perish. He camped on the west bank of the Angelina and corresponded with Bowles, whom he found friendly and extremely eager to have the line marked off. He reported that he had asked Bowles to send him help from his people, which Bowles did. In nineteen days the line, he said, had been run without molestation by thirty-four whites and sixteen Cherokees. The line extended from the Neches River to the Angelina, thence to the first large creek below the main Shawnee village, thence up that creek to its source, thence due north to the Sabine River. Horton concluded his report to Houston:

> You may be sure that everything that art, villainy, corruption and treachery could invent were resorted to, to break down and destroy the expedition, but all in vain. We have succeeded and all are home safely and the Indians are all well satisfied and will remain in peace if the whites will let them alone.[28]

26 *Ibid.*, 201.
27 *Ibid.*, 199.
28 McClendon, "First Treaty," *loc. cit.*, 43.

That was the last action Houston delegated in regard to the Indians. He could do no more for his Cherokee friends. He had been a great and steadfast friend, but his term had expired, and Mirabeau Buonaparte Lamar was elected president. The new cabinet had made the boast that they would kill off Houston's pet Indians.[29] Lamar wanted the Indians expelled from Texas. He did not believe that they would uphold a treaty.[30] In his inaugural address, he said that the sword would mark the boundaries of the Texas Republic.[31]

[29] Starr, *History of the Cherokee Indians*, 223.
[30] Muckleroy, "Indian Policy," *loc. cit.*, Vol. XXVI, 128.
[31] Homer S. Thrall, *A Pictorial History of Texas from the Earliest Visits of European Adventurers to A.D. 1879*, 117. Hereafter cited as *Pictorial History*.

CHAPTER VIII

Houston, Lamar, and the Cherokees

Mirabeau Buonaparte Lamar was well versed in Indian issues when he went to Texas. A native of Georgia, he had witnessed his state's defiance of the federal government in the dispute over Indian lands. He had served as the personal secretary of the stern, proud Governor George M. Troup and had been living in the Troup home when Creek Indian lands in Georgia were expropriated for the benefit of white settlers under the guise of states' rights. It was natural that the young and impressionable Lamar would be strongly influenced by the Georgia governor and would absorb many of his convictions. When he left for Texas, Lamar carried with him a hostility against the Indians and a strong faith in the doctrine of states' rights.[1]

Many persons, including Lamar, thought that the treaty with the Cherokees was a "nullity" from the beginning.[2] In his presidential message to congress on December 21, 1838, Lamar said, "It is not necessary to inquire into the nature and extent of the pledge given to the Cherokees by the Consultation of 1835 and the Treaty of February, 1836 . . . for the treaty was never ratified by any competent authority."[3]

David G. Burnet, acting secretary of state under President

[1] Charles P. Roland, *Albert Sidney Johnston: Soldier of Three Republics*, 14–15. Hereafter cited as *Albert Sidney Johnston*.

[2] *Lamar Papers*, II, 590–92.

[3] Starr, *History of the Cherokee Indians*, 218–19.

Lamar, wrote Richard G. Dunlap, Texas minister in Washington, on May 30, 1839, urging him to use his influence in persuading the American government to recall the Indians from Texas. Burnet expressed President Lamar's views when he wrote that the Provisional Government itself, under whose authority the treaty "purports to have been made, was acting without the sphere of any legitimate power and could not . . . impose any moral or political obligation upon the independence and separate Government of Texas." He also wrote that Horton had run the boundary lines designated in the treaty without authority, since the senate had advised against it.[4]

Most historians have agreed that the treaty was legal. Yoakum wrote, "The idea that the Consultation had no power to make such a pledge was preposterous." The Texans violated the pledge first: "The ink was scarcely dry on the treaty paper when locators and surveyors were seen in the forest."[5] Their presence was unlawful according to the decree of November 13, 1835, in which the Consultation had ordered all locations and surveys stopped.

Houston bitterly ridiculed the idea that the Consultation had no power to pledge the faith of the nation and no power to dispose of any part of the public lands:

> They had *all* the power at the time. . . . there was no other government or authority recognized in the country. . . . we might as well say that the Consultation had no power to borrow money, or pledge the faith of the nation in any other matter, as to say she had no right to make this pledge to the Indians.[6]

In 1842, when he was again president of Texas, Houston wrote Texas Attorney General G. W. Terrell, asking his opinion about the Cherokee title to lands in East Texas. Terrell replied that the Cherokee claim had been a legal one. He pointed out that intruders had been driven off the lands during the Mexican

[4] *Lamar Papers*, II, 590–92.
[5] *History of Texas*, II, 266.
[6] Houston, *Writings*, II, 323–47.

Artist's conception of Chief Bowles. Sketched by Grayson Harper.

This photograph was captioned "Richard Fields" in Clarence R. Wharton's *Texas under Many Flags*. It is probably not the old chief but his eldest son, who bore the same name.

Sam Houston, a powerful and steadfast friend of the Cherokees. Reprinted from Homer S. Thrall, *A Pictorial History of Texas*.

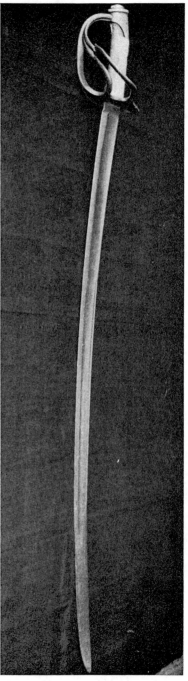

The elegant sword presented to
Chief Bowles by Sam Houston is
now on view at the Tahlequah,
Oklahoma, Masonic Lodge.

The treaty of February, 1836, bears the signatures of Sam Houston and John Forbes and the marks of Chief Bowles, Big Mush, and others. Courtesy Texas State Archives, Austin.

Stephen F. Austin, "Father of Texas," thought the Cherokees deserved their land. Courtesy Fort Worth Public Library.

Killough Monument near old Larissa, north of Jacksonville, Texas.
Courtesy R. F. Moore.

Site of the Killough Massacre, which occurred on October 5, 1838, the largest single Indian massacre in East Texas. Many Texans blamed Chief Bowles and his tribe for the crime. Courtesy R. F. Moore.

administration, an action which proved that Cherokee settlement rights were recognized by the Mexican government. He believed that, by settling and continuously occupying their lands, the Cherokees had acquired an inchoate right to them, which should have matured into a perfect title.

In commenting on the treaty made by the Consultation of Texas with the Cherokees in 1836, Attorney General Terrell agreed that all members had signed it in good faith and added: "They were the only political authority known to the country for the time being and were therefore necessarily charged with the duties and attributes of Government. They were the government de facto."[7]

But those opinions were voiced some years later, long after the Cherokee question had reached its tragic climax. During Lamar's tenure as president of Texas, Indian atrocities, suspected intrigue between the Cherokees and the Mexicans, and defiance by both groups of the Texas government convinced Lamar that the Cherokees had to go. Most Texans agreed with the new president. He hoped that they could be evicted peacefully.[8]

The situation had become tense before Houston's term ended. Rumors that Bowles had given Vincente Córdova, a Mexican revolutionary, permission to operate in Cherokee territory caused further mistrust of the chief.[9] There is little doubt that Córdova wooed Chief Bowles with glowing promises, as shown by the following letter, dated July 19, 1838, from Córdova to Manuel Flores, a Mexican Indian agent in Matamoros:

> I hold a commission from General Vincente Filisola to raise the Indians as auxiliaries to the National Army and I have already entered upon my duties by inviting a meeting of the neighboring tribes . . . being informed that you are appointed for the same

[7] Memorandum to Governor John Connally Concerning Cherokee Indian Claim Relating to Lands in Texas, Appendix A, Opinion of Attorney General G. W. Terrell to President Sam Houston of the Republic of Texas in reference to Cherokee Lands, City of Houston, September 10, 1842, Attorney General's office, Austin, Texas, 1–9.

[8] *Lamar Papers*, II, 590.

[9] Winfrey, "Chief Bowles of the Texas Cherokee," *loc. cit.*, 36.

purpose . . . I hope you will make every effort to approach with such force as you may have at your command, and that you will bring the pipe, which I understand you are in possession, in order that the Indian chiefs may smoke it of the Cherokee and other tribes, who have promised me to unite as soon as possible for action, and who have also agreed that in case our plans should be discovered in the meantime, they then will commence operations with the force we may have at command. . . . It is highly desirable that you should approach to give us in such a case a helping hand. . . . I desire we should treat with each other in full confidence which is necessary to the success of our commission.[10]

In August, 1838, it was learned that six hundred Mexicans and Indians under the command of Vincente Córdova, Nathaniel Norris (the former alcalde of Nacogdoches), and others were encamped on the Angelina River. Bowles was rumored to be in league with them. A proclamation was issued ordering them to return home and lay down their arms. The rebels replied:

The citizens of Nacogdoches, being tired of the unjust treatment and of the usurpation of their rights, can do no less than state that they are embodied with arms in their hands, to sustain their rights and those of the nation to which they belong. They are ready to shed the last drop of their blood; and declare as they have heretofore done, that they do not acknowledge the existing laws through which they are offered guaranties for their lives and properties.[11]

The paper was signed by Córdova and eight others.

This reply unquestionably signified an armed rebellion against the constituted authorities. Thomas Jefferson Rusk of Nacogdoches, major general of the Texas militia,[12] immediately enlisted a company of about seven hundred volunteers to quell the

---

[10] Winfrey *et al.*, *Texas Indian Papers*, I, 8.

[11] DeShields, *Border Wars of Texas*, 293–94.

[12] *Journal of the House of Representatives of the Republic of Texas, 1838*, Annual sess., 175. A bill was passed to organize the militia, and Rusk was appointed adjutant general. Houston vetoed the bill because it took the appointment of the adjutant general out of his hands.

uprising. Rusk's first move was to find the rebels. It was reported that they were heading toward the Cherokee Nation. Rusk, who wanted no trouble with Bowles, wrote the chief a letter merely reporting that some Mexicans, who had always been treated well by the Americans, had killed, had stolen horses, and were threatening war. They had, he said, run away like cowards when pursued by the Texans and had taken refuge in Bowles's nation. Rusk added that President Houston had sent a messenger to talk with Bowles but that the Mexicans had not permitted him to go to Bowles's home. Rusk asked Bowles to reveal the Mexicans' hiding place. He assured the chief that he had no plans for his forces to pass near Indian women and children, since it might make them uneasy. He assured Bowles:

> We have collected a number of our warriors to chastise these men as they deserve. We are friends of your people and do not intend any harm to them. You may assure them that if they remain peaceable and quiet we will do them no harm. We believe the talks you have had with us and that you are our friends. Between the houses of friends there ought to be a plain path, but it is wrong to allow our enemies to come into your nation.[13]

Rusk sent his letter by an aide, Joseph Durst, accompanied by an escort of several militiamen.

Durst brought back disturbing news to Rusk's camp. He had talked with Chief Bowles, Big Mush, and the Mexicans, all of whom were armed and apparently ready for attack. They had agreed to postpone any action until ten o'clock the following morning, when Rusk's representatives would meet them at the home of Ellis P. Bean, the Mexican Indian agent.

Rusk immediately wrote President Houston, who was then in Nacogdoches:

> This Sir, is your matter, not mine. Left to my own opinions, ten o'clock tomorrow would find my whole force at them if not earlier.

---

[13] Thomas Jefferson Rusk Papers, East Texas Room, Paul L. Boynton Library, Stephen F. Austin State University, Nacogdoches, Texas.

> Retrieve yourself by twelve o'clock tonight, or I shall march up there with my whole force and not wait to talk much with a set of infernal scoundrels who have meditated the death of women and children without provocation, but I shall certainly not give evidence of want of subordination.

Rusk's letter revealed his impatience with the president, who had been issuing orders from Nacogdoches and was not fully aware of the situation in the field, as Rusk was. In a second letter written on the same day Rusk wrote to Houston: "Had I jumped on the Mexicans as I intended at first this matter would have been settled in my opinion. . . . I wish this infernal question of war or peace with the Cherokees was settled. It embarrasses my operations greatly."[14]

Rusk wrote to Chief Bowles again on August 15 from his camp on the Angelina River. He told the chief that the trail of the Mexicans led toward the Cherokee village and that the enemy had boasted that the Cherokees would join them. "I believe this is false," he wrote. He told Bowles that he would pass near his nation with a force of troops on the next day but would not harm his people. "Remain at home in peace and you will not be disturbed. Do not let the Mexicans come among you," he warned.

The next day Rusk wrote Houston that the Mexicans were camped about two miles from Bowles's home and that the Cherokee chief was holding talks daily in the enemy camp. Rusk also complained that the Mexicans were preventing communication between him and Chief Bowles:

> This state of suspense is rather irksome to me. I wish to avoid the imputation of raising an Indian war on one side while I do not like to incur the charge of remaining idle until our enemy has had time to make all his arrangements and concentrate his forces. . . . I shall attempt a communication with Bowles today and inform him that we have no disposition to do him or his people harm but that a hostile force must not remain without giving privilege to me to follow them.[15]

[14] *Ibid.*   [15] *Ibid.*

In the meantime, President Houston, still in Nacogdoches, had become seriously concerned about the assumed Indian-Mexican alliance. Fearful of an attack on Nacogdoches, he asked Rusk to send troops to guard the town. Rusk replied that he would immediately send a part of his force to Nacogdoches if there was any danger but that he was sure that there was none since his scouts had not reported any movement by the enemy in that direction.[16]

Houston wrote a final letter to his old friend Bowles:

My Brother, when I wrote to you last I hoped that trouble would have ended. It has not been so. . . . I am told the enemy are in your village. . . . They must not stay in your country or it will make trouble. . . . Two thousand men on Red River are ordered under arms, and the United States soldiers and cannon on the Sabine are called for under the treaty, and will come. . . . In ten days we will have more than one thousand men here and I hope to the Great Spirit that my red brothers will not make war nor join our enemies, for if they gain a little now they must soon lose it all, and ruin will come upon them and their people. Remember your words spoken to me, and my words to you shall stand for I lie not to my red brothers. Be at peace and happy. General Rusk says if you are peaceful that you shall not be hurt nor your people. Remember me and my words. We have not asked you to join us to make war, but to remain at peace.[17]

Hoping to keep the peace with the chief, President Houston ordered Rusk not to cross the Angelina River when following the Mexicans and Indians.[18] His final note to Rusk advised: "If the Bowl means to compromise with the enemy, accept such terms as will give honorable peace to the country. God prosper you, and I only wish you may soon put an end to the war."[19]

Rusk, however, thought it best to pursue Córdova's force.

[16] *Ibid.*
[17] Houston, *Writings*, II, 277.
[18] Dudley G. Wooten (ed.), *A Comprehensive History of Texas, 1685 to 1899*, I, 335.
[19] Houston, *Writings*, II, 276.

Despite President Houston's order he led his men into the Cherokee Nation, an act that for a time, alienated the two men who had been close friends.

When Rusk and his army arrived at Bowles's village, Córdova's revolutionaries had disbanded and escaped. Chief Bowles declared his innocence of any part in the plot.[20] It was thought that Córdova and his followers had gone to the Kickapoo village, in what is now northeastern Anderson County. The Kickapoos had been the first to break the peace with Bowles, a peace he had kept since 1817. In 1835 they had attacked a family living on Cherokee lands. Bowles had declared them renegades and had no longer recognized them as members of the Indian community.[21] The Kickapoo village seemed a logical refuge for the Mexicans.

On August 18, after the militia returned from the Cherokee Nation, President Houston issued the following order to the troops:

> The brave men who will have so promptly rallied to their country's defense, it is hoped, will soon be discharged and will return to their homes. They have done all that it was possible for them to achieve under the circumstances! The enemy are now dispersed, but not without some expectation that they may again unite at some point so as to annoy a portion of our population. The troops in falling back, or returning, will treat the Indians and their property as its guardians; preventing all injury to every species of property. This especial request is made of the gallant officers and by the President with a confident hope that his old companions in arms will not disregard his solemn request. I salute the army.[22]

The order demonstrates Houston's consideration for Chief Bowles and his people. But Houston was widely criticized for his restraint. On August 26, Colonel Hugh McLeod, aide to

[20] Jack Moore, *The Killough Massacre*, 13.
[21] A. M. Gibson, *The Kickapoos: Lords of the Middle Border*, 152.

Thomas J. Rusk, wrote Vice-President Lamar, giving him a report of the rebellion:

> [The Mexicans'] designs are no longer questionable, but for the accidental explosion of the plot before it was matured, every tribe of Indians in Eastern Texas would have been engaged in it . . . had they not been alarmed by the sudden appearance of General Rusk with upwards of seven hundred men. . . . General Rusk's movements prevented, I have no doubt, a general Indian war. . . . none of the mainsprings of the affair . . . are yet taken. The President was in town during the difficulties. . . . he cramped General Rusk in every way with his orders, written here, where he could not judge what was the true state of affairs.[23]

Houston replied to Rusk's charges in his farewell address to congress in November, 1838. He condemned Rusk for encroaching on the presidential power during the Córdova rebellion. He also censured the Texas congress for limiting presidential power to defend the country by placing the authority for financial matters entirely in Rusk's hands.[24]

Rusk's large militia force was discharged after returning to Nacogdoches, as President Houston requested. But in October, 1838, Rusk again mobilized the militia and with 250 men rode to the Kickapoo village where the Mexican rebels were said to be hiding. Colonel McLeod described what followed in a report to newly elected President Lamar. Rusk and his men attacked the village early on a rainy morning when the air was full of mist. Rusk advanced twenty paces and shouted, "You damned cowardly . . . , come out and show yourselves like men." The firing then began, and Rusk and his men soon routed the rebels, killing eleven men, one of them a Cherokee named Tail. No Texans were killed, although most of them had their clothes ripped by bullets, and they lost thirty-five horses. The enemy

---

[22] *Lamar Papers*, II, 206.

[23] *Ibid.*, 209.

[24] *Journal of the House of Representatives of the Republic of Texas*, Regular sess., 3d Cong., 1839; William Kennedy, *Texas: The Rise, Progress, and Prospects of the Republic of Texas*, II, 316.

forces, numbering 250, according to McLeod, included Mexicans, Negroes, Caddoes, Coushattas, Keechis, and others.[25]

When Rusk returned home, he wrote to Bowles about Tail's death and warned him to keep his warriors away from the enemy: "Our people are enraged at the innocent blood that has been shed and are using every quarter to punish our enemies. . . . if you act as our friends and have nothing more to do with our enemies, you and your people have nothing else to fear from us."[26] Bowles replied only that he had never been able to manage Tail, that he was a bad Indian and "was well killed."[27]

In August of that critical summer a Mexican, Pedro Julián Miracle, was killed on Red River. A diary and papers found in his possession proved that he was a member of the insurgents. This further evidence of the enemies' schemes added fuel to the fire, especially when it was learned that one of the papers was headed "Private Instruction for the Captain of Friendly Indians of Texas, by His Excellency General in Chief Vincente Filisola."[28] The papers also instructed Miracle to urge the Indian chiefs to take up arms against the whites and to give them gifts of lead and tobacco. After the campaign was over, the warriors would be permitted to go to Mexico to pay respects to the Mexican government, which would send a commissioner back with them to give each man the land to which he was entitled.

The ruthless murders of the Killough family on October 5, 1838, the largest single Indian massacre in East Texas, stirred the entire Republic of Texas, and hatred flamed against the Indians. Eighteen members of that large family, including married sons and daughters and their children, who had come to Texas from Alabama in 1837, were brutally murdered near the settlement of Larissa, in present Cherokee County. The deed was committed inside the Cherokee Nation, and many Texans

[25] *Lamar Papers*, II, 265–67.

[26] *Ibid.*, 255.

[27] *Ibid.*, 265–67.

[28] Christian, "Mirabeau Buonaparte Lamar," *loc. cit.*, Vol. XXIV, 47–48.

blamed Chief Bowles and his tribe for the crime.[29] Bowles protested the Cherokees' innocence and claimed that roving bands of prairie Indians had killed the family.[30] It is highly probable that some of the wild tribes aligned with Córdova killed the Killough family, but, whether innocent or guilty of the murders, the crime put Chief Bowles and his people on the whites' blacklist.

After the Killough tragedy little concern was shown for Cherokee rights in Texas. Old promises were forgotten. Most citizens longed for the day when the Indian menace would be removed. The saga of the Cherokees in Texas was drawing to a close.

After his narrow escape in the Cherokee Nation, Córdova, the wily Mexican leader, made his way to the wild Indian tribes on the upper Trinity and Brazos rivers.[31] In March, 1839, he departed for Matamoros with about seventy-five men to confer with Canalizo, who had succeeded Filisola as commander there, about obtaining military supplies for the Texas uprising.[32]

Settlers from the Hornsby settlement (near present Austin, Texas), looking for stolen horses, discovered the trail of the Mexicans. Believing that Indians were raiding near the settlements, they organized a ranger company to pursue them. Colonel Edward Burleson served as commander, and Captains Billingsley and Andrews each headed a company. There were about 150 men in the party. The Texans overtook the renegade army in a post-oak grove near Seguin. Colonel Burleson formed his men in a V. Captain Andrews commanded the right wing; Captain Billingsley, the left. At the first volley the enemy fled, and a running fight followed. About eighteen of Córdova's men were killed, but he escaped and eventually returned to Mexico with his surviving followers.[33]

Chief Bowles continued to deny that he had allied himself

[29] Moore, *The Killough Massacre*, 4–20.
[30] Woldert, "The Last of the Cherokees in Texas," *loc. cit.*, 207.
[31] Thrall, *Pictorial History*, 58.
[32] DeShields, *Border Wars of Texas*, 294.
[33] J. W. Wilbarger, *Indian Depredations in Texas*, 153–57.

with Córdova, though his people had been urged to do so. Albert Sidney Johnston, Texas secretary of war, did not believe Bowles,[34] and warned the chief against collusion with the enemies of Texas. In a letter dated April 10, 1839, he told the chief that the Texas congress would soon adopt measures that would render abortive "any attempt to again disturb the quiet of the frontier . . . and that all intercourse between the friendly Indians and those at war with Texas must cease."[35]

In April or May, 1839, Manuel Flores, the Mexican Indian agent at Matamoros, started for Texas with a large pack train and a plan to meet Córdova. About thirty men, Mexicans and Indians, were included in his party. Among them were some renegade Cherokees from Bowles's nation.[36] Flores had about 150 horses and mules, most of them well loaded with supplies, ammunition, and arms.

Flores had also been ordered by Canalizo to deliver important papers to Córdova, detailing plans for overthrowing the Anglo-Texans. In addition Flores carried letters addressed to Bowles and Big Mush which appeared to implicate the chiefs in the plot.[37]

It so happened that while Flores was en route a ranger company led by Captain Mike Andrews and Lieutenant James O. Rice was out on a scouting mission. They found the Mexican agent and his party camped in a cedar brake on Onion Creek, south of present Austin. Because the Mexicans and Indians were hidden among the brush and timber, it was impossible to tell how many there were in the party. Flores' men put up a bold defense, daring the rangers to attack them. One civilian, Wayne Burton, urged Captain Andrews not to attack, and some of the men did return to the settlement at Hornsby.[38]

[34] Roland, *Albert Sidney Johnston*, 90.
[35] *Lamar Papers*, II, 522–23.
[36] Wisehart, *Sam Houston*, 351.
[37] Woldert, "The Last of the Cherokees in Texas," *loc. cit.*, 207.
[38] Wilbarger, *Indian Depredations in Texas*, 157–64.

About twenty Texans followed the Mexicans, traveling over such rough country that many of their horses were soon lamed. Finally Captain Andrews had to turn back, and the Texans who kept up the pursuit were forced to travel slowly to conserve their horses. A hard rain dimmed the trail but in time they reached the San Gabriel River where they found a campfire recently abandoned by the Mexicans.

Encouraged, they rode ahead and soon saw the Mexicans in front of them. Flores made a stand as if to fight, but the wild yells of the Texans put him in retreat. Finally Flores and about ten of his men did make a stand on a bluff overlooking the San Gabriel River. They fired a volley but missed the Texans. In return fire William Wallace shot Flores through the heart. Seeing their leader dead, Flores' men quickly rode away, leaving their camp equipment, baggage, ammunition, and pack animals behind them.[39]

Official correspondence from Canalizo was found in a leather sack on Flores' body. A few of the Texans knew enough Spanish to realize that the letters were of great importance. They lost no time delivering them to Secretary of War Johnston, who forwarded them to President Lamar.[40] Included in the papers were letters addressed to Bowles and other Indian chiefs, promising them their lands if they would make war against Texas.[41] Those letters spelled the doom of the Texas Cherokees. In another captured dispatch Canalizo had promised Córdova that the Mexican army, greatly strengthened, would recover Texas as soon as hostilities with France, which had attacked Veracruz, were ended. The Indians were urged to harass the Texans in any manner possible—burn their homes, destroy their fields, and steal their horses and cattle. The chiefs were told that "they need expect nothing from the greedy adventurers for land who

[39] *Ibid.*
[40] *Ibid.*
[41] Roland, *Albert Sidney Johnston*, 91.

wished to deprive them of the sun that warmed and vivified them, nor from those who would not cease to injure them while the grass grew and water ran."[42]

President Lamar and most Texans were convinced that the time had come to end the Cherokee "menace" in Texas. When it was learned that some Cherokees were in Flores' party, still more hatred was stirred against "Old Bowles," as the chief was now referred to by the angry whites. Lamar's followers charged that the Indians had represented Bowles in negotiations with Santa Anna.[43]

Was Chief Bowles guilty of collaborating with the Mexican revolutionaries? Houston never believed that he was. "If the Mexicans saw proper to open a correspondence with him, must he be punished for receiving the letter?" he asked.[44]

In later years Yoakum wrote that the Mexican leaders had only slight acquaintance with Chief Bowles.[45] The manner in which the papers were addressed to Bowles and Big Mush would lead one to believe that Córdova did not know the correct titles of his alleged allies. Big Mush was addressed as Chief while Bowles was given the title of Lieutenant-Colonel.[46] The correspondence proved only one thing: the Mexicans, realizing that the Cherokees were by far the most advanced Indian tribe in Texas, hoped to have them on their side in war against the Texans.

In later years Walter Prescott Webb agreed with that view, commenting that "there is a lack of evidence that the Cherokees did more than listen with Indian politeness to the warlike proposals of the Mexicans."[47]

Few people held such views at the time, however. Secretary of

---

[42] Wilbarger, *Indian Depredations in Texas*, 152.
[43] Wisehart, *Sam Houston*, 351.
[44] Houston, *Writings*, II, 323–47.
[45] Winfrey, "Chief Bowles of the Texas Cherokee," *loc. cit.*, 37.
[46] Burton, "The Cherokee War," *loc. cit.*, 37.
[47] *The Texas Rangers*, 53.

War Johnston expressed his sentiments in a warning letter to the chief in April, 1839:

> ... recent developments go to show incontestably that the Cherokees, or a portion, the Delawares, Shawnees, Kickapoos ... etc, entered into a compact with Cordova to carry on war as soon as he should return with supplies from Matamoras. ... This design has been happily prevented by the destruction of Cordova's party and perhaps Cordova himself. The President grants peace to them but is not deceived. They will be permitted to cultivate undisturbed as long as they manifest by their forbearance from all aggressive acts ... or until congress shall adopt such measures in reference to them as in their wisdom they may deem proper, with a clear view of all matters connected with their feelings and interests. It should not surprise the Cherokees to learn that such measures are in progress under the orders of the President as will render abortive any attempt to again disturb the quiet of the frontier nor need it be any cause of alarm to those who intend to act in good faith, all intercourse between the friendly Indians and those at war with Texas must cease. The President directs that you will cause the contents of this communication to be made known to all the chiefs present at the council.[48]

Lamar wrote to Shawnee chiefs in June, 1839, telling them of the Cherokees' treachery—how they had listened to the lies of the Mexicans and how they had foolishly sworn their faith to the faithless. He concluded:

> The Cherokees can no longer remain among us. ... They must return to the land appropriated by their great father, the President of the United States for the permanent residence of their people. ... I hope they go in peace and return no more; for we have no wish to shed the blood of the red men. ... You are not Cherokees ... be admonished and refrain from all collusion with them.[49]

When news of the captured letters spread through Texas,

[48] *Lamar Papers*, II, 5–22.
[49] *Ibid.*, III, 11–12.

tempers flared and fears of Indian uprisings were rampant. Lamar sent Major B. C. Waters to eastern Texas in May, 1839, with two companies to occupy the Neches Saline.[50] They were to keep an eye on the Cherokees and prevent them from meeting with Indians from the west, the Caddoes, Coushattas, Comanches, Tawakonis, and others. The Neches Saline was in Cherokee territory. Chief Bowles, indignant at the president's order sent word to Major Waters that the Cherokees would meet him with force if he occupied the territory. Major Waters dared not risk a fight with Bowles and wisely decided to establish his headquarters on the west bank of the Neches, outside Cherokee country.[51]

An editorial in the *Houston Telegraph* on June 19, 1839, was typical of the reactions of most Texans to Bowles's threat:

It is rumored that the Cherokee whose machinations with our Mexican enemies have been long suspected and are now so fully developed have recently shown unequivocal symptoms of hostility . . . that they have refused, with sufficient audacity, to be sure, to permit the establishment of a military station on the Great Saline [Neches] and have even ordered our citizens to decamp from the grounds which they pretend to claim by virtue of a treaty . . . made with them by certain commissioners under the late Provisional Government. We have neither time nor inclination to discuss the preposterous absurdity of that so-distant treaty. It has never been ratified, has received no sanction except from the inexplicable fatuity of the commissioners who made it. To confirm it now, would inflict irreparable injury to Texas and positive palpable injustice upon her citizens. . . . Shall the Cherokee, an insignificant renegade band of savages be permitted to put at naught the authority of the country and, in spite of ourselves, to establish an *imperium* in *imperie*, in the very heart of our republic?

President Lamar was outraged when he learned that Bowles

---

[50] Winfrey, "Chief Bowles of the Texas Cherokee," *loc. cit.*, 37.
[51] Woldert, "The Last of the Cherokees in Texas," *loc. cit.*, 200.

had defied the government order. He wrote to the chief immediately:

> I have learned with much surprise that you have ordered Major Waters from the Great Saline. In this, you have committed an error. That officer was acting under the authority and orders of this Government and any attempt on your part, either by force or threats, to impede the execution of his duty, cannot be regarded by the executive in any other light than as an outrage upon the sovereignty of the nation. . . . The forked tongue of the Mexicans has beguiled you; and you are running into dangerous paths contrived by the enemies of Texas for our injury and your ruin. . . . Neither is the Government ignorant of the fact that a secret understanding has existed between you and the traitor Cordova. . . . He is our open enemy and known to be your confidential friend and counsellor. . . . The Cherokee will never be permitted to establish a permanent and independent jurisdiction within the inhabited limits of this Government. . . . the political and fee-simple claims which they set up to our territory now occupied, will never be allowed. If they remain at home . . . without murdering our people, stealing their property, or giving succor and protection to our enemies, they will be permitted to remain in the undisturbed enjoyment of their present possession until Congress shall be able to make some final arrangements, satisfactory to both parties, for their return to their own tribes beyond the Red River.[52]

Recalling earlier days, President Lamar also accused Chief Bowles of having gathered his warriors on the San Antonio Road east of the Neches during the "Runaway Scrape" three years before and of planning to attack the settlers if they were defeated by Santa Anna. Lamar dispatched the letter to Chief Bowles by Martin Lacy, Indian agent, who was accompanied by Dr. W. C. W. Jowers, John H. Reagan, and a half-blood Mexican interpreter named Cordray.[53] It was to have tragic results.

[52] *Lamar Papers*, II, 590.
[53] Reagan, "Expulsion of the Cherokees," *loc. cit.*, 38–46.

CHAPTER IX

The Cherokee War

JOHN H. Reagan, who later served as a justice of the Texas Supreme Court, a United States senator from Texas, and the first chairman of the Texas Railroad Commission,[1] was an enthusiastic young newcomer to Texas in 1839, when he accompanied Indian Agent Martin Lacy to Chief Bowles's home. Reagan's report of that historic visit to the old chief has been widely quoted by past and present historians. He was deeply moved by all that he saw and heard. His sympathy was with Bowles from the beginning.[2]

Reagan wrote that when he and the other three men—Lacy, Jowers, and Cordray—rode into the Cherokee village and to the chief's home, the latter, who had heard the horses approaching, was standing in the doorway barelegged and bareheaded. Recognizing Lacy, he greeted the men and motioned to them to dismount. He led them to a deep, cool spring[3] behind his cabin and invited them to sit down upon a dead tree.

Lacy delivered President Lamar's letter to the chief. Bowles

---

[1] Walter Prescott Webb *et al.* (eds.), *The Handbook of Texas*, II, 443–44.

[2] Reagan, *Memoirs*, 29–36; Reagan, "Expulsion of the Cherokees," *loc. cit.*, 38–46.

[3] In 1923, Albert Woldert visited the spring, on the Tillman Walters survey a short distance northwest of Redlawn and about four miles northwest of Alto, Texas. Woldert found it on the western side of a small red hill, neglected but still flowing. "Last of the Cherokees in Texas," *loc. cit.*, 198. From Reagan's account it appears that the Cherokee village was nearby. "Expulsion of the Cherokees," *loc. cit.*, 38–46.

carefully inspected it a few seconds, then gave it to Cordray to read and interpret. Reagan wondered what thoughts lay behind the stoic face of the aged chief as he listened to Lamar's words. Surely he realized that this was the ultimatum. His people would have to go or fight the Texans. What would follow, peace or war?

After hearing the contents of the letter, Bowles stood straight as a sapling before his guests, his sunburned, wrinkled face a mask. There was a quiet dignity in his tall frame and noble bearing. Through the interpreter he told Lacy that he could not reply to the letter until he had talked with his headmen. He said that he had been corresponding with John Ross, principal chief of the Georgia Cherokees, about a proposed removal of all the Cherokees to California where they would be entirely out of reach of the white people. He asked Agent Lacy to come back in ten days for his answer. Lacy agreed to do so, and he and his companions rode away, leaving Chief Bowles by the spring.

When the ten days had passed, Lacy rode back to talk with Chief Bowles, accompanied by the same companions.[4] Bowles again led them to the spring and, speaking through Cordray, told the agent that his young warriors wanted war and believed that they could whip the Texans. Bowles, too, believed that his warriors could eventually defeat the whites but said that it would take at least ten long years of bloody, frontier war. He and Big Mush did not want war, he said, but added that, though he differed from the younger chiefs, he would lead them against the Texans because he had led them too long to step down now. He recalled how he had led them first to the St. Francis country of Missouri, then to Lost Prairie in Arkansas, and later to the Three Forks of the Trinity (now Dallas). He had hoped to hold the Three Forks country, but after several years of warfare with prairie Indians and the loss of a third of his warriors, he had been forced to settle near Nacogdoches.[5]

Chief Bowles denied the charges Lamar had made against his

[4] *Ibid.*
[5] *Ibid.*

people. He said that the wild tribes had committed the murders and the thefts. He defended the right of his people to the East Texas land, reminding his hearers that he had journeyed to Mexico to secure title and that Houston had confirmed their rights in the treaty of 1836.[6]

Chief Bowles said further that he was an old man of eighty-three and that in accordance with the ways of nature, he would not live much longer. That did not worry him, he said, but he was greatly concerned for his three wives and his children.[7]

The old chief appeared fatalistic in his conversation with Lacy.[8] He said that if he fought the whites they would kill him, and that if he did not fight them his braves would kill him. Reagan was greatly impressed by the respect and understanding that Chief Bowles and Agent Lacy displayed toward one another, commenting that, though neither man could read or write, enlightened diplomats could not have handled the situation with more tact or patience.

After Lacy and his companions reported the news that the Cherokee chief and his warriors would fight for their rights, President Lamar appointed Vice-President David G. Burnet, Secretary of War Johnston, General Rusk, Major James S. Mayfield, and I. W. Burton as commissioners to represent the Texas Republic in dealing with the Cherokees.[9] He wrote to the newly appointed commissioners on June 27, 1839:

Recent events of which you are already apprised convince me of

[6] *Ibid.*

[7] *Ibid.* It is not known exactly how many children Chief Bowles had. One daughter, Rebecca, married Tessee Guess, the son of Sequoyah. Bowles told members of the Maverick family that he had given one of his daughters to Houston, evidence that he had more than one daughter. When accepting the commission from the Mexican government after the Fredonian Rebellion, Chief Bowles had offered to give two of his small sons to Mexican authorities to be educated in Mexico. An older son, John, was heir apparent as the chief. See Woldert, "The Last of the Cherokees in Texas," *loc. cit.*, 188; Starr, *Old Cherokee Families*, 366; Winkler, "The Cherokee Indians in Texas," *loc. cit.*, 153; John Henry Brown, *Indian Wars and Pioneers of Texas*, 68.

[8] Reagan, *Memoirs*, 29–36.

[9] DeShields, *Border Wars of Texas*, 300.

the necessity of the immediate removal of the Cherokee Indians, and the ultimate removal of all other emigrant tribes now residing in Texas. . . . I have therefore appointed you commissioners . . . to make the necessary arrangements for carrying this measure into effect. . . . It is desirable that this should be done in a peaceful and friendly manner, and to render the proposition acceptable to the Indians, you are authorized to make them a fair and liberal compensation for their improvements . . . crops and such other property as they will be unable to take with them out of the country. . . . You will not agree to pay them more than one-fourth in cash, the residue to be paid in goods which is understood the merchants of Nacogdoches and San Augustine will advance at fair prices on the credit of the government. . . . In no event will you agree to pay a larger sum than twenty-five thousand in cash . . . under no circumstances can they be permitted to remain in the country longer than will be required to make the necessary preparations for their removal . . . and unless they consent at once to receive a fair compensation for their improvements and other property and remove out of this country, nothing short of the entire destruction of all they possess and the extermination of their tribe will appease the indignation of the white people against them.[10]

After receiving the president's letter, the commissioners sent the following one to Colonel Bowles and other chiefs of the Cherokees:

The undersigned have been appointed by the President, commissioners to arrange with you the removal of the Cherokees from the territory of Texas. . . . We wish to be just, even to the weak whom we can easily destroy, and we are therefore willing to make you ample compensation for the improvements you have made in our country and to pay you for the corn which you may leave on the ground provided you and your people will retire in peace and return no more to Texas. Come and see us and we will talk more fully on this subject. Colonel McLeod will give you and as many

10 Winfrey *et al.*, *Texas Indian Papers*, I, 67–70.

of your head men as you choose to bring, safe escort to our camp and our young men will not molest you.[11]

In the letter Secretary Johnston also stated that unless the Cherokees signified their willingness to submit to the orders of the government within a specified time they would be attacked.[12]

General Rusk's East Texas regiment was the first to arrive upon the field.[13] He was accompanied by Secretary Johnston and Adjutant General Hugh McLeod (appointed by President Lamar on January 20, 1839). Camp Johnston was established in the extreme southwestern corner of present Smith County. Bowles's camp was several miles away on Council Creek. Negotiations were carried on for several days.[14]

An incident that occurred a few days before the actual fighting began could have wrought havoc upon the whites, who were not yet up to battle strength. John Bowles, the chief's son, and a few companions crossed the neutral line which had been established between Bowles's camp and the Texas troops. Chased away by the Texans, John and his companions rode back to the Cherokee camp and reported that they had been attacked. Much excitement prevailed until satisfactory explanations were made to Chief Bowles.[15] He calmed his warriors and prevailed on them not to attack the whites—another instance in which the old chief displayed good judgment and determination to fulfill all agreements honorably.

In the meantime, the commissioners had drawn up the following articles of agreement to submit to Chief Bowles:

> Article 1. The Cherokees and their associate bands agree to depart from the Territory of Texas and separate in peace and friendship with the people thereof.
>
> Article 2. It is agreed that the commissioners will pay the Cherokees and others on the part of the Government of Texas, a

[11] Rusk Papers, *loc. cit.*
[12] *Ibid.*
[13] Woldert, "The Last of the Cherokees in Texas," *loc. cit.*, 210–11.
[14] *Ibid.*
[15] Reagan, "Expulsion of the Cherokees," *loc. cit.*, 38–46.

full and just compensation for their improvements, crops . . . and all other property that they may leave through necessity or choice, the prices and valuation of the same to be agreed to and determined by the appraisers who have been appointed by the President and selected by Colonel Bowles for that purpose. The payment to be made in goods and cash in such a manner and in such proportions as may be agreed upon by the parties hereto.

Article 3. It is agreed that the removal of the Indians shall take place as easily as the necessary arrangements can be made therefor, and in the manner herein pointed out. The Government will furnish provisions and supplies to destitute families on the march from the Territory of Texas.

Article 4. It is also stipulated that as soon as the valuation of the property is effected, that the goods shall be paid over to the Cherokees and others for which the commissioners shall issue the necessary orders, and the money that may be due will be paid over as soon as they reach the territory of the United States.

Article 5. It is stipulated that the Cherokees and those who may remove with them shall be escorted to the United States line, that they and their property may be protected from the wild Indians and by such a force as the Secretary of War may direct.

Article 6. It is likewise agreed that the Indians will not disperse without permission from the commissioners and shall encamp where they may direct, until the tribes are ready to move, the officers to have free access to the camp at all times.

Article 7. It is also agreed to avoid all difficulty and misunderstanding that the Indians shall encamp separately and sentinels shall be placed between to prevent our men from entering and mixing in their encampments. Some of the Texans would march in company and encamp with the Indians as a guarantee that no harm is intended, or will be permitted to be done to them on their march.

Article 8. It is also stipulated and agreed as a guarantee that the Cherokees and others will act in good faith and remove peaceably and not violate their friendly agreement, that they will allow the locks to be taken off all their guns except fifty which shall be taken good care of and returned to them as soon as they reach the United States.

Article 9. The same arrangements will be made with the Shaw-nees and Delawares. Those of said tribes who are now ready to go with the Cherokees will be allowed to do so, and those who are not ready to go will be escorted in the same manner as is above stipu-lated by such a number of troops as the Secretary of War may direct, and as soon as like arrangements can be made for them.[16]

On July 11 the commissioners and Indians met at Council Creek. Chief Bowles represented the Cherokees; Spybuck spoke for the Delawares. About twenty-five Indians and two inter-preters, Hill and Cordray, were present. Rusk spread blankets upon the ground for the chiefs. Secretary of War Johnston said to Bowles:

When I last saw you at Houston I did not expect to meet you again under the circumstances we now meet. Still, not withstanding the course you have taken with the Mexicans and our enemies, it depends on you whether we part in peace or not. . . . The Presi-dent has received your talk through Mr. Lacy . . . and I now come to arrange for your departure. The President, in view of all the circumstances has determined that we must separate. He prefers peace to war and desires that you should go in quiet, influenced by that spirit of justice which should be found in the heart of the ruler of civilized people. . . . He has made arrangements to pay you a fair price for your improvements and all the property you may leave behind.

Vice-President Burnet then addressed Bowles:

. . . we have conquered the country from the Mexicans. It is ours. Mexicans and our people cannot live together in peace. . . . The Mexicans are our enemies and the Cherokees are their friends. They have protected Mexican traitors, to wit Cordova and others. For these reasons the President believes that we cannot live together here in peace. Therefore the Cherokees had better go away. . . . The President desires peace but is always ready for war. The Cherokees are few whilst the Texans are like leaves on the trees, and are daily increasing from the United States. They had

[16] Rusk Papers, *loc. cit.* The quotations that follow are also from the Rusk Papers.

better go in peace to that place where they will be protected and remain at peace, than stay here where they will be destroyed.

General Rusk spoke next. He said that it was greatly against the interest of both parties to fight, that neither side would gain anything and both would lose. The whites would lose a great deal, and the Cherokees would lose all. Many would be killed on both sides, and the cries of women and fatherless children would call upon the Great Spirit for vengeance on the head of him who unnecessarily began the war. He told the Cherokees that they were once a powerful people but had been reduced to a small band by war and would be reduced still further by more wars. Rusk assured Colonel Bowles that he did not wish to injure him or his people and would not do so unless forced to action. He reminded the chief that he had marched seven hundred men through the Cherokee Nation during the past summer and had done the tribe no harm. He told Bowles that it was impossible to be friendly both to the Texans and to their enemies, the Mexicans and wild Indian tribes. "If you remain in friendship with the wild Indians and Mexicans we will be forced to kill your people in defense of our frontier," Rusk warned. "You are between two fires and if you remain will be destroyed." He told Chief Bowles that the object in holding the councils was to make a friendly arrangement and that there was no necessity for the Indians to display war clubs and paint their faces black. "It is our wish to settle our difficulties peaceably," he stressed.

Chief Bowles then rose to speak. He was thankful, he said, to hear the truth and would agree to what the commissioners said. He had heard that the Texans were going to fight the Cherokees. His women and children were in poor condition. He said that he would submit the talk to his people and return the answer the next day. "I hope that when we come to a fair understanding it will all be the truth. I do not want either party to be deceived," he said.

A second meeting was held on July 12. Chief Bowles began

the talks by saying that it was a fine day and that the Great Spirit would bear witness that what he might speak was the truth, and for good. Yesterday he had said little; today he would speak more fully. What he said would be sanctioned by his people. Big Mush was not present but would agree to all that Bowles said. His young men's minds had been disturbed but were now at rest, and he hoped that what he did today would make all right. He said that he pitied the condition of his women and children if war broke out. He would move his families and people, and they would part in peace and friendship. They would return over the road whence they had come. He asked that three moons' time be granted to him before the removal and promised that all the Indians would go, including his people, the Shawnees, Alabamas, Coushattas, and Delawares. All of their young men would go as soon as they could get supplies but that they had no ammunition to kill game and some delay would be necessary. His people would not return to their houses, for the women and children would be loath to leave them when the time came. It would be best to return only to gather corn and make arrangements for the journey. "I have said all that is necessary for the present," the old chief concluded.

Spybuck then spoke for the Shawnees. He said that his people were also willing to go and asked that the Indians be allowed to remain for two moons. "In that time our women can get all ready."

Rusk concluded the conference by agreeing with Bowles that it *was* a good day and that the Great Spirit would look down with satisfaction upon the arrangement:

> I am glad that the matter is now about to be arranged peaceably. It is greatly the best for both parties. Had we gone to war, women and children would have suffered. As it is with this friendly arrangement they will live in peace and not be afraid.

Before the meeting was adjourned, the Cherokees were told that the three moons' delay could not be granted, but ample time to make every preparation for removal would be given, and supplies would be furnished to those families who were destitute. Another meeting was planned in two days' time, when Big Mush and the Delaware chief could be present.

On July 14 the commissioners met the Indians for the third conference. Before the meeting began, Rusk once again spread blankets. This time, however, Bowles said that he preferred to sit on the ground. After being urged several times, he acquiesced, but another chief, Key, refused to do so.

Burnet then read the articles of agreement which the commissioners had written. After Cordray had translated the articles for Bowles, the old chief said that he was opposed to marching out of the country escorted by troops. He had come into the country alone and wished to depart the same way. Otherwise, it would look as though he were a prisoner. He objected strenuously to giving up the gunlocks and said that that point should have been mentioned to him sooner. He said his warriors would also oppose it.

The commissioners then told Chief Bowles that many white people had no confidence in the chief's words and required him to sign a treaty as proof of his sincerity. When Bowles refused to do so, they reminded him that in 1835, when the Indians were holding friendly talks with the whites, they were also in correspondence with General Cos, the commander of the Mexican army. Moreover, they said, after the Battle of San Jacinto, Bowles had sent some of his men to hold friendly talks with the enemy in Matamoros. They reminded him that a Mexican officer had visited the Cherokee Nation during the past summer to confer with the Indians and that Córdova and the Mexicans had sought refuge in the Cherokee Nation.

> All these things we know and it is repeated to you for no other purpose than to show you we have no right to place confidence in your word. How can we know if we pay you and let you go, that you will not go on to the western frontier and join the enemy. We are in earnest and to show it we place some of our best men

in your camp. We would not give the lives of these men for all your gunlocks, but in order that this matter shall be carried out correctly, and not fail, we require this pledge of you.

The stubborn old chief still refused to sign the treaty, at least until he had counseled with his warriors again. He promised to give his answer in a day or two. He thought that they would agree to the terms.

That night the commissioners no doubt discussed the situation until a late hour. All of them sensed that something was wrong. Chief Bowles had not shown the same friendliness on the third day of the council meetings as he had shown at first. His reluctance to sit on the blanket spread by Rusk was a marked sign of hostility. Could Chief Bowles really be trusted? Was he delaying matters on purpose to gather his forces? What were his absent chiefs doing? Why had Big Mush been absent from all the meetings?

The next morning Major Mayfield, Colonels McLeod and Williams, John Thorn, and James Durst proceeded to Bowles's camp, hoping that he would sign the treaty. They reached the Indian headquarters about eight o'clock and found Chief Bowles there with about eighty warriors.

Mayfield talked with Bowles through Cordray. Bowles admitted that he was having much trouble with his young men. Their minds were much disturbed, and their women were afraid. Many men had run away, unwilling to give up their gunlocks. They believed that the Texans would kill them as soon as they released their weapons.

Mayfield then told Chief Bowles that the Texans wanted no further delay, that some action had to be taken. He urged the chief to settle the matter about the gunlocks, and then everything could be arranged. He suggested that the chiefs present could sign the treaty then and the absent ones could sign later, since Bowles had assured the commissioners previously that Big Mush and the other chiefs would do what he, Bowles, wanted them to do. The old chief then called his warriors together for a conference under a near-by shelter, where he talked seriously for a good while. He finally returned, only to tell Mayfield that his warriors would not sign the treaty.

Mayfield then warned the chief that the Texas Army would move out that day and urged Bowles to go with him and talk once more with the commissioners. Bowles turned and walked away. Mayfield was hopeful that he was going for his horse, but the chief spoke again with his warriors. After a short time, he told Mayfield that he could not ride with him to the Texas camp.[17]

Old Chief Bowles was a shrewd leader. It is seriously doubted that he ever considered signing the white man's treaty of removal from his vast, rich territory in East Texas. If he had once considered doing so, the clause providing that the Indians give up their gunlocks may have caused him to change his mind. There is no doubt that he encountered stiff opposition from the younger braves to that provision. Chief Bowles was probably playing his final card with the Texas government, and that card was time. His attendance at the council meetings, where decisions were continuously delayed, may have been a ruse. Certainly Secretary Johnston and others feared that the chief was delaying matters to give the Indians time to mobilize their warriors for battle.[18] The fact that many of Chief Bowles's warriors, including Big Mush, were absent from the council meetings, could mean only one thing: they were rounding up the braves from associated and wild tribes to come to the aid of the Cherokees.

Chief Bowles was not the only one playing for time during those uncertain days. The Texans too were awaiting reinforcements.[19] They had learned from their scouts about a large number of Indian warriors, perhaps as many as eight hundred, gathering in the area of Bowles's camp. Rusk's forces were not large enough to battle that many braves.[20] It was imperative that

[17] *Ibid.*
[18] Roland, *Albert Sidney Johnston*, 92.
[19] Reagan, "Expulsion of the Cherokees," *loc. cit.*, 38–46.
[20] Woldert, "The Last of the Cherokees in Texas," *loc cit.*, 212.

Colonel Burleson's regiment and Colonel Landrum's regulars arrive before the battle was joined. Burleson had been on the Colorado River collecting forces to operate against the Indians when he had received orders to march with his men on East Texas.[21] He and Landrum arrived with their troops on July 14.[22]

Soon after Mayfield and his companions returned to the Texans' camp, Chief Bowles, his son John, and Fox Fields, carrying a flag of truce, rode to the Texas camp and gave notice that they would move west of the Neches River later that morning. Bowles was told that the Texas forces would also break camp and follow the Indians.[23]

The Texans, chafing in the blistering July heat, were eager to pursue the Indians. General Kelsey H. Douglass of the Texas militia, now in command of all forces, ordered the men to ride toward Bowles's encampment. Landrum crossed over to the west side of the river with his men, to meet the Cherokees if they turned in that direction. That move prevented him from taking part in the first battle with the Indians.

Burleson and Rusk with their men headed directly to Bowles's camp, only to find it empty. Following the well-marked trail for about six miles, they found the Indians late in the afternoon. The Indian forces were on the point of a hill near the Delaware village. Rusk motioned the Indians forward. They advanced a short distance, yelling and firing their rifles, and then took refuge in a thicket covering the bottom of a ravine. The Texans charged the ravine and quickly killed eighteen warriors, putting the rest to rout in wild confusion. Two Texans were killed outright; a third one was mortally wounded. By that time night had fallen, and further fighting was impossible.[24]

[21] Wilbarger, *Indian Depredations in Texas*, 171.

[22] *Ibid*.

[23] Reagan, "Expulsion of the Cherokees, *loc cit*., 38–46.

[24] *Lamar Papers*, III, 45–47. Douglass to Johnston, *Niles' National Register* (Baltimore), August 10, 1839, fifth series, Vol. VI, No. 24. This paper carried letters from General Douglass to Albert Sidney Johnston taken from the *Redlander* (San Augustine, Texas) of July 20, 1839, and a letter from Rusk to that newspaper reporting the news of the battle to the citizens.

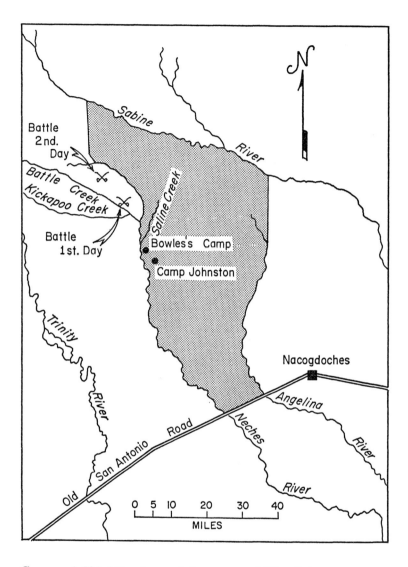

Camps of Chief Bowles and Secretary of War Johnston before
and during the Battle of the Neches.

Adapted from Charles P. Roland, *Albert
Sidney Johnston: Soldier of Three Republics*

Before making camp, the Texans gathered the booty they had captured from the fleeing Indians. There were five kegs of powder and 250 pounds of lead, many horses, cattle, corn, and other supplies.[25] The ample supplies of powder and lead were proof that belied Chief Bowles's claim that the Indians lacked ammunition. Not many Texans slept that night. Most of them remained on guard. Others rode back to protect outlying settlements from marauding and vengeful Indians.

On the next day, July 16, the Texans again formed ranks and set out in pursuit. They passed the Delaware village and left it in flames. They soon came upon a mile-long line of warriors near the Neches River in present Van Zandt County. Both sides attacked, and the fighting continued for an hour and a half. It ended in the Neches bottom. The Indians' losses were large. There was blood everywhere.[26]

Chief Bowles, mounted on a handsome sorrel horse with blazed face and four white feet, was almost alone upon the field when he gave the signal to retreat. Reagan, describing the scene, said that Bowles clutched the sword that Houston had given him and wore the bright silk vest and sash, also gifts of Houston, his friend and brother. A black military hat was upon his head.[27] Reagan was greatly impressed with the old chief's bravery. Throughout the battle his voice could be heard urging his warriors on. Now, in that moment of defeat, Reagan wrote, he was "a magnificent specimen of barbaric manhood."[28]

Bowles's horse, which had been shot several times, fell to the ground, throwing off his rider. The chief slowly rose to his feet, and as he started to walk away he was shot in the back by Henry Conner. Bowles took a few steps and fell, then rose to a sitting position facing Reagan's company. Reagan described the dramatic scene:

[25] Reagan, "Expulsion of the Cherokees," *loc. cit.*, 38–46.

[26] *Lamar Papers*, III, 46–47. Douglass to Johnston.

[27] Reagan, *Memoirs*, 29–30.

[28] *Ibid.*

I had witnessed his dignity and manliness in council, his devotion to his tribe in sustaining their decision against his judgment, and his courage in battle. Wishing to save his life I ran towards him. As I approached from one direction, my captain, Robert Smith, approached him from another with his pistol drawn. I said, "Captain, don't shoot him," but as I spoke he fired, shooting the chief in the head which caused instant death.[29]

Reagan excused Smith's action. His captain, whom Reagan called a worthy citizen, had known of many murders and thefts by the Indians. It was possible that in the heat of battle he did what under other circumstances he would not have done. It was also said that Smith killed Bowles because the old chief had killed his father-in-law.[30]

The sword was taken from the dead warrior's hand and presented to Smith.[31]

In 1885, C. N. Bell, who served under Captain Smith in the battle, gave his own version of the chief's death:

Chief Bowles was wounded in the battle and after this Captain Smith and I found him. He was sitting in the edge of a little prairie on the Neches River. The chief asked for no quarter. He had a holster of pistols, a sword and a Bowie knife. Under the circumstances the captain was compelled to shoot him as the chief did not surrender nor ask for quarter. Smith put his pistol right to his head and shot him dead.[32]

John Henry Brown wrote that at least a half-dozen men boasted that they had killed the famous chief. "The inquisitive

[29] *Ibid.* In his book *Mirabeau Buonaparte Lamar, Troubadour and Crusader,* Herbert Pickens Gambrell disagrees with Reagan's report. He wrote (p. 243) that Bowles killed himself by plunging a sword into his heart. It is likely that Reagan's account is the accurate one.

[30] Winfrey, "Chief Bowles of the Texas Cherokee," *loc. cit.,* 32n.

[31] James, *The Raven,* 309. Captain Smith donated the trophy to the Masonic Lodge of Henderson, Texas. It was later given to Colonel James H. Jones, who carried it in the Civil War. About 1890 it was presented to the Cherokee Nation. It is now owned by the Tahlequah, Oklahoma, Masonic Lodge. It is in good condition and highly prized. Woldert, "The Last of the Cherokees in Texas," *loc. cit.,* 233.

[32] Brown, *Indian Wars and Pioneers of Texas,* 68.

mind will fail to see the compulsive necessity of killing the disabled chief when his slayer was enabled to put his pistol 'right to his head and shot him dead,' " he commented.[33]

The body of Chief Bowles was mutilated after his death. One "ghoulish wretch" cut strips of skin from the old chief's back, saying that he planned to make them into bridle reins.[34] According to an article in the *Telegraph and Texas Register* of September 1, 1841, "Some rude chaps scalped the poor chief after his death." According to tribal custom, funeral honors were paid only to unscalped braves.[35] Perhaps that explains why the Indians left Chief Bowles's body on the battlefield. An early settler in the area, Tom Ingram, could see the skeleton of the Cherokee chief near the Neches River when he hunted or fished in the area. He said that the skull remained for many years near the spot where the chief had died.[36]

Sorrow and disorder followed his death. Big Mush had also been killed in battle. The retreating warriors made their way to Bowles's camp. All that night the victorious Texans, camped nearby, heard a moaning noise as the Cherokees readied for their journey and mourned their dead. When the sun came up the following morning, the camp was empty. The Indians were gone; they had vanished like the early morning mist on the Neches. Mooney wrote:

> Some of them went to Arkansas; others to Indian Territory bringing with them the bloodstained canister containing the patent for their Texas land which Bowl had carried about with him since the treaty with Houston and which he had upon his person when he was shot.[37]

After the short, final struggle, General Douglass wrote his

[33] *Ibid.*

[34] Noah Smithwick, *The Evolution of a State; or, Recollections of Old Texas Days*, 280.

[35] C. L. Douglas, *Cattle Kings of Texas*, 183.

[36] Mildred Stanley, "Cherokee Indians in Smith County," *Texas History Teachers Bulletin*, Vol. XII, No. 1 (Oct., 1924), 124–25.

[37] *Myths of the Cherokee*, Pt. I, 145–46.

General Thomas J. Rusk, whose regiment was the first to arrive upon the field before the Battle of the Neches. Reprinted from Dudley G. Wooten (ed.), *A Comprehensive History of Texas, 1685 to 1899.*

Edward Burleson had a prominent part in the Battle of the Neches. Reprinted from Dudley G. Wooten (ed.), *A Comprehensive History of Texas, 1685 to 1899*.

David G. Burnet, first president of Texas, participated in the Cherokee
War. Courtesy Barker Texas History Library, Austin.

Albert Sidney Johnston served as secretary of war during the Cherokee War. Courtesy Library of Congress.

Mirabeau Buonaparte Lamar, under whose administration the Cherokees were defeated and driven out of Texas. Reprinted from Dudley G. Wooten (ed.), *A Comprehensive History of Texas, 1685 to 1899.*

ON THIS SITE THE

CHEROKEE
CHIEF BOWLES

WAS KILLED ON JULY 16, 1839 WHILE
LEADING 800 INDIANS OF VARIOUS
TRIBES IN BATTLE AGAINST 500
TEXANS · · THE LAST ENGAGEMENT
BETWEEN CHEROKEES AND WHITES
IN TEXAS

Erected by the State of Texas
1936

Monument marking the spot where Chief Bowles was killed. Courtesy
Morris S. Burton, Tyler, Texas.

Monument and battleground on the Neches Plain, where Chief Bowles
was killed and his warriors were defeated. Courtesy Morris S. Burton,
Tyler, Texas.

A view of the Neches River near present Tyler, Texas.

report to Secretary of War Johnston, telling him that "the notorious Mexican ally, Bowles," had been killed.[38] "All Texans behaved so gallantly it would be invidious to particularize," he added.[39]

The Battle of the Neches, fought during the hot July days of 1839, was one of the most important engagements ever fought on Texas soil. It ranks second only to the Battle of San Jacinto. Eight hundred warriors fought nine hundred well-armed Texans.[40] In addition to Bowles, "the Moses of their tribe,"[41] over one hundred warriors fell. Of the Texans, five men were killed and twenty-seven were wounded.[42] But they had achieved what they fought for—the red man's land.

The Texans followed the Indians' trail for about ten days, burning their villages and homes as they came upon them. They appropriated enough Indian corn to supply the army in that part of the country for a year.[43] As his men left a burning trail behind them, General Douglass observed the beauty of the country. He said, "It would vie with the best portions of Texas."[44] On July 25 the troops were disbanded, and the men rode home. Their work was done.[45]

As the Cherokees were crossing the Red River into Indian Territory, a party of hunters fired upon them, killing four of their number.[46] That was their farewell from Texas.

[38] Starr, *History of the Cherokee Indians*, 220.

[39] *Lamar Papers*, III, 45–47.

[40] Roland, *Albert Sidney Johnston*, 93. Wilbarger wrote in *Indian Depredations in Texas*, p. 172, that there were eight hundred Indians in the conflict and five hundred Texans. Winfrey cites the same number in "Chief Bowles of the Texas Cherokee," *loc. cit.*

[41] Brown, *Indian Wars and Pioneers of Texas*, 68.

[42] Woldert, "The Last of the Cherokees in Texas," *loc. cit.*, 199.

[43] *Telegraph and Texas Register*, Houston (Aug. 14, 1839).

[44] Starr, *History of the Cherokee Indians*, 221.

[45] Wilbarger, *Indian Depredations in Texas*, 172.

[46] Webb, *The Texas Rangers*, 54.

CHAPTER X

"Not Without Shades of Sorrow"

Nᴏᴛ all of the Cherokees returned to the United States after they were driven from East Texas. John Bowles, who became chief after his father's death, and Egg, a lesser chief, tried to lead a remnant of their defeated people across Texas into Mexico late in the fall of 1839. From there they planned to make raids into Texas to harass the whites who were responsible for their sorrow and misery.[1] They moved toward their destination in a roundabout manner, always avoiding white settlements. They camped for a while at the headwaters of the Trinity River, northwest of present Fort Worth,[2] and then made their way in a southwesterly direction toward Mexico. Colonel Edward Burleson, who had helped defeat the Cherokees on the Neches, was making a winter campaign between the Brazos and Colorado rivers. On Christmas Day, 1839, he and his men encountered John Bowles and his party near the mouth of the San Saba River in present San Saba County. The Indians fired as soon as they saw the Texans. Many of them, including John Bowles and Egg, were killed by return fire in the short, fierce battle that followed. John's mother, two sisters, and three children were taken prisoner.[3]

[1] Brown, *Indian Wars and Pioneers of Texas*, 69.
[2] Wilbarger, *Indian Depredations in Texas*, 172.
[3] Brown, *Indian Wars and Pioneers of Texas*, 69.

When John Bowles was killed, he was wearing the large black military hat that Chief Bowles had worn when he was killed.[4] No doubt he had gone back to the battlefield on the night of his father's death and retrieved the hat, along with a pair of pistols and a Bowie knife which Chief Bowles was said to have been carrying[5] and which were never accounted for.

After the battle Colonel Burleson found a three-cornered hat among the plunder. It was no doubt the hat that the Mexican officials had presented to Bowles after the deaths of Chief Fields and Hunter. Thinking that Houston had given it to Chief Bowles, he sent it to Adjutant General McLeod, asking him to deliver it to Houston. His letter to McLeod read:

> Sir, I send my Lieutenant Moran with the cocked hat of the distinguished friend of General Sam Houston, Colonel Bowles, and as it first emanated from him I specially request you to present it to him from me as compliment.

McLeod delivered the hat to Houston, who took the gift as a personal affront not only to himself but to congress. He denied having given the hat to Bowles and introduced a resolution in the house of representatives asking the president to dismiss McLeod from office. He argued for its passage in a bitter, hourlong speech.[6] Houston's indignation is understandable. He felt that both Burleson and McLeod were ridiculing the old chief and making light of the friendship and loyalty that Houston had always felt for the Cherokees. The former president's feelings about this subject ran too deep to be taken lightly. The storm finally cooled, however, and McLeod remained in office.

After John Bowles was killed, many of his group escaped to Mexico. Burleson and his men captured a number of women and children and perhaps some older warriors. The Indians were held prisoners in Texas. In April of the following year the Cherokee National Council met in Fort Gibson, Indian Territory, and

---

[4] Wisehart, *Sam Houston*, 352.
[5] Brown, *Indian Wars and Pioneers of Texas*, 68.
[6] This incident was reported in the *Texas Sentinel* (Austin) on June 15, 1840.

asked General Matthew Arbuckle, who commanded the Second Western Division of the United States Army there, to write a letter to President Lamar requesting that all their people still held in Texas be returned to their nation, where they would thereafter remain.

Branch T. Archer, secretary of war of the Texas Republic, answered the letter on July 11, 1840:

> . . . we have suffered and are still suffering most serious injury from the intrusive advances of the Cherokee people within the limits of our jurisdiction and territory. The position in which we stand to the Cherokee people within our limits, is hostile; we should therefore be greatly pleased to see them returned to their legitimate home and again reunited with their own people in the United States. The Cherokee prisoners have been dispatched to the post most convenient to our command. . . . We trust that within thirty days from this date they will be at Fort Jessup, La.[7]

The Cherokees who escaped to Mexico settled in a village near the small town of San Fernando. In 1842, Sequoyah, the remarkable Cherokee who devised an alphabet for his people, left his home in Indian Territory and with companions journeyed overland to Mexico, where he visited this band of former Texas Cherokees. (It will be remembered that one of Chief Bowles's daughters had married a son of Sequoyah.) Sequoyah died in the Cherokee village in 1843. His death was certified by Chief Standing Bowles and two companions at Warren's Trading House on Red River in 1845.[8] (Whether Standing Bowles was a younger son or a grandson of old Chief Bowles is not known, but there is no doubt that he was a direct descendant, or he would not have inherited the chieftaincy.)

It is not known how long the Cherokees lived in Mexico. In 1843, the year Sequoyah died, about thirty members of the tribe, in a distressed condition, were encountered on the treaty

---

[7] Starr, *History of the Cherokee Indians*, 222.

[8] Grant Foreman, "The Story of Sequoyah's Last Days," *Chronicles of Oklahoma*, Vol. XII (March–December, 1934), 25–41.

ground at the Texas frontier by General Edward H. Tarrant and Captain Booth, who had been appointed to negotiate a treaty of perpetual amity with ten tribes of Indians at Bird's Fort on the Trinity River. On October 14, 1843, the Clarksville *Northern Standard* carried a report about the Cherokees. They were members of Chief Bowles's Texas Cherokees and included members of the old chief's family. They had been robbed of all their possessions by the Mexicans and were without clothing or horses. The Cherokees would not leave their camps to talk with the commissioners until clothes had been provided for the women and children. "Accustomed to the decencies of life they were unwilling to show themselves to civilized people in their state at that time," General Tarrant reported.

The chiefs of many tribes put their marks upon the treaty signed at Bird's Fort on September 29, 1843. Among them were the leaders of the Delaware, Chickasaw, Waco, Tawakoni, Keechi, Caddo, Anadarko, Ioni, Biloxi, and Cherokee tribes. Tarrant and G. W. Terrell signed for the Texas Republic. A Cherokee captain named Chicken Trotter put his *X* on the treaty for the Cherokee people.

The treaty contained twenty-four articles. Among the most important were the first two. Article 1 read:

> Both parties agree and declare that they will forever live in peace and always meet as friends and brothers. Also that the wars which may have heretofore existed between them shall cease and never be renewed.

Article 2 read:

> They further agree and declare that the Indians will never unite with the enemies of Texas nor make any treaty with them, which shall require of the Indians to take part against Texas.[9]

The town of Cherokee and Cherokee Creek in San Saba

---

[9] Winfrey *et al.*, *Texas Indian Papers*, 241–46. It should be noted that the *Northern Standard* lists General Edward H. Tarrant and Captain Booth as the commissioners who signed the treaty and that *Texas Indian Papers* lists Tarrant and G. W. Terrell as the signers.

County, Texas, were named in memory of that last defeated remnant of the Texas Cherokees.

Most Texans in all walks of life, from the humble colonist on the frontier to the highest officials of the republic, justified the war with the Cherokees and drew sighs of relief when they and their associate bands were driven from the country. From the first it had been inevitable that the Indians would be removed or destroyed. The entire western frontier was in constant danger of depredations by the wild tribes. Despite the fact that the Cherokees were considered civilized by many, and, according to Houston "had never drawn one drop of white man's blood,"[10] they were Indians, and the white settlers wanted them out of Texas.

Perhaps never before had so many high-ranking government officials fought upon a battlefield. Vice-President Burnet, who was acting president while Lamar was absent on a visit to the United States, was present. Albert Sidney Johnston, secretary of war, was also there, as was Adjutant General Hugh McLeod. Each of them received minor wounds.[11] General Thomas J. Rusk, who had served as secretary of war during the interim government and later as head of the Texas militia, was a participant, as was Colonel Edward Burleson, who would become vice-president of the republic under Houston in 1841.

President Lamar naturally justified the war. He saw the Cherokees as enlightened and wily foes who, through their superior intelligence, wielded a great influence over the wild Indians. Although the Cherokees were an immigrant tribe, they had asserted political rights. He remained convinced that they had committed atrocities against the settlers and had been in secret agreement with the Mexicans.[12]

In a speech in Galveston in June, 1840, Lamar referred to the Cherokees:

[10] *Writings*, II, 320.
[11] Brown, *History of Texas*, II, 163.
[12] *Lamar Papers*, III, 165.

The expulsion of the Cherokees, for which the executive has been made the subject of so much unmerited vituperation was a measure which the safety and tranquillity of the country imperiously demanded.[13]

And at another meeting in Houston the president made a similar speech, vindicating his part in the Cherokee removal and expressing his satisfaction that Bowles, "the chief agent in the foul machination against us, atoned for his perfidy with his life."[14]

Lamar's reference to "unmerited vituperation" was undoubtedly a reference to Houston's reaction to the Cherokee War. Former President Houston was away from Texas on a visit to Andrew Jackson when the war took place.[15] He was furious when he learned of it. Upon his return to Nacogdoches he reviewed the Indian campaign in a savage speech. Since many Nacogdoches citizens had been in favor of the war and had fought in the struggle, they did not relish Houston's criticism and accused him of inciting the Indians to resist the government. Angry threats were made against Houston's life, and he was told that he would be shot if he tried to speak. Houston spoke nevertheless. He denounced the administration for breaking faith and accused the soldiers of barbarously mutilating the body of the old Cherokee chief.[16] Houston said that Bowles was "a better man than his murderers."[17] His heated speech estranged some of his close friends, including Rusk, Adolphus Sterne, and Henry Raguet.

Houston and Burnet were candidates for the presidency in 1841, and the campaign was a bitter one.[18] Newspapers of the period were filled with letters from supporters of both candidates. A letter in the September 1, 1841, *Houston Telegraph*, from a Nacogdoches citizen, showed that the writer had not forgotten Houston's bitter speech after the Cherokee War. He

[13] *Ibid.*, 401. [14] *Ibid.*, 397.
[15] James, *The Raven*, 308.
[16] Alfred Mason Williams, *Sam Houston and the War of Independence in Texas*, 252.
[17] James, *The Raven*, 309.
[18] Mary Whatley Clarke, *David G. Burnet, First President of Texas*, 186–210.

wrote that Houston's characterization of Bowles as "a better man than his murderers" was nonsense, that no thinking man would vote for Houston, and that if Houston was elected he would use his power to pass his "infamous Cherokee bill" to avenge the death of his friend Bowles. The writer added that the Indians had turned the garden spot of East Texas into a wilderness.

Johnston became a Texas hero and was commended by President Lamar for "his vigor in pressing the war." Testimonial dinners were held in his honor, praise poured in from all over Texas. From the beginning Johnston had agreed with President Lamar about the Cherokees. He believed that self-government made them a nation within a nation and thus a menace to the republic. He said that their domain separated the eastern section of the country from the western and the north from the south and that their possession of the rich East Texas lands had kept white settlers from the area.[19]

Houston was especially bitter toward Johnston for the prominent part he had played in the war. Rumors spread that Houston was making malicious and insulting remarks about Johnston. When the secretary of war heard the rumors, he sent a note to Houston, telling him that he would hold him accountable for his words. Houston denied the rumors and said that nothing had transpired within his knowledge "which could change the estimation, which I have always entertained of the high and honorable bearing of General Johns[t]on, and his character." The two men were outwardly friendly when they met in the future but "smouldered inwardly with distaste for each other."[20]

As long as Houston lived, he felt strongly about the removal of the Cherokees. He never forgave the Lamar administration for evicting Bowles's people from Texas and never lost an opportunity to express his outrage at the treatment they had received. In the congressional debate of December 2 and 3, 1839, when the

[19] Roland, *Albert Sidney Johnston*, 94.
[20] *Ibid.*

removal of the capital to Austin was discussed, Houston opposed the move, saying that the country was wild and far from civilization, that the savage Indians could come and burn the town, take the public archives at any time they pleased, and murder the inhabitants. He added:

> The friendly Cherokees, who had formed a barrier between the people of the east and the wild Indians, and protected them, have been driven from their homes. They are equal to the Americans, man to man; they could meet and fight them, and the blood of a Bowl is still unburied! . . . But they have a right to be heard as much as those who located their hundred leagues of land around Austin . . . the Government has acted towards them in bad faith.[21]

Houston then calmed down a bit and said he would speak no longer on the Cherokee subject at that time but that before congress adjourned he would put the Cherokee campaign in the right place, "where it would stick like a blister."[22] He always remembered Chief Bowles with affection and admiration and considered him the hero of the whole ugly episode. He would have agreed heartily with historian Walter Prescott Webb, who wrote that Chief Bowles "acted nobly during the struggle and died like a gentleman."[23]

Houston paid a final tribute to the memory of his Cherokee friends by keeping their rich lands from the hands of land-grabbers. He made a determined and successful fight in congress to see that the Cherokee lands reverted to the republic and that the proceeds from their sale went to the hard-pressed Texas treasury. He introduced a bill providing that the land be divided into 640-acre tracts and offered for sale. In January, 1840, the bill was passed by a large majority, and exploitation of the Cherokee claim ceased.[24]

After the danger from Indians was ended, Texas began to

[21] Houston, *Writings*, II, 316–18.
[22] *Ibid.*
[23] *The Texas Rangers*, 54.
[24] Wisehart, *Sam Houston*, 351.

prosper. Government finances improved, and loans were much easier to obtain from the United States.[25] Would-be settlers, who had been afraid to move into the Texas wilderness because of the Indians, now moved to the republic.

Thus closed a blood-stained and tragic chapter in Texas history. The once-proud Texas Cherokees had become a broken and dispirited minority of the Cherokee Nation in Indian Territory. Their rich lands were no more. Their story was a re-enactment of the age-old struggle between advancing civilizations and those who resist. Only in particulars was the Cherokee tragedy unique. The acts of political connivers, desperate Indians, and land-hungry settlers made it inevitable that blood would flow and the innocent be killed. It was "not without shades of sorrow" that the Cherokee story ended at last in a struggle simply for self-preservation.[26] Moreover, many historians agree with Webb who wrote that "it is extremely doubtful if history will justify the measures adopted by the Texans against the Cherokee Indians."[27]

It is an ironic note to history that Chief Bowles of the Texas Cherokees may have been the single most important man in Texas' struggle for independence. Had he not kept his people neutral, the Battle of San Jacinto might have had a far different outcome. It was tragic that his final reward from the Texans was death for himself and expulsion for his people.

[25] Roland, *Albert Sidney Johnston*, 94.
[26] Brown, *Indian Wars and Pioneers of Texas*, 68.
[27] *The Texas Rangers*, 54.

CHAPTER XI

Cherokee Claims to Texas Land

Ever since the Cherokees were defeated and driven out of
Texas in 1839, they have sought payment for their East Texas
lands, which they claim were ceded to them by both Mexico and
Texas. Those lands today constitute one of the richest areas of
the state of Texas. They contain productive oil fields and for-
tunes in lumber, salt, and industry.

Around 1913–14 a real-estate broker, C. C. Metheny, was
employed by descendants of Richard Fields to push the Cherokees' claim to lands in Smith, Cherokee, Van Zandt, Nacogdoches, and Rusk counties. He was to receive 25 per cent of the
proceeds. Metheny wrote at least thirteen letters to John M.
("Appletree") Smith, who had married into the Fields family,
regarding claims to Texas lands. That dream drifted away; lack
of funds prevented Metheny from going to Mexico City to
gather the official data needed for pressing the claim against
Texas. According to T. L. Ballenger, the letters are still in the
possession of Smith's descendants.[1]

In 1920, George W. Fields, signing as "representative and
attorney of the Texas Cherokee and Associate Bands," instituted
an unsuccessful legal action to regain the Cherokee lands in
Texas or in lieu thereof to obtain other lands in Texas.[2] In

[1] T. L. Ballenger Papers. Newberry Library, Chicago.
[2] Samuel E. Asbury Folder, East Texas Room, Paul L. Boynton Library,
Stephen F. Austin State University, Nacogdoches, Texas.

November, 1921, descendants of the Texas Cherokees filed a petition with the United States Supreme Court, requesting permission to file an original bill against the state of Texas for the recovery of one and a half million acres of land. They claimed that the territory of the Western Cherokees was a foreign state and that the tribe had the right to sue Texas for recovery of those lands. Their request was refused; the court ruled that the Cherokee Nation was not a "foreign state" in the sense in which that term is used in the Constitution. The court's decision was based on the case of the state of Georgia against the Cherokees.[3]

In 1948 a Cherokee claim for thirty million dollars was filed against the federal government at Washington, D.C. The Texas Cherokees did not claim mineral rights to the territory, which by that time had become one of the world's richest oil fields. They wanted five million dollars, the estimated realty value as of January 1, 1840, and 5 per cent interest from that date. The Cherokee attorneys pressed their case before the Indian Claims Commission, which had been set up in 1946 to weigh and recommend for final settlement claims totaling billions of dollars based upon treaties and agreements between the Indians and the whites.

The Cherokee claim was based on an agreement signed between Captain Richard Fields for the Cherokees and Governor Trespalacious of the province of Texas in 1822, and upon the treaty signed by Houston and Forbes and the Cherokees in February, 1836. By the wording of the treaty the Texans had granted the Cherokees "the right to occupy and enjoy their lands forever."

The petition claimed that admission of Texas to the Union had the legal force and effect of extending the sovereignty of the United States over all the lands and citizens of Texas and that redress was due.[4] That claim was also denied.

The most recent petition regarding Cherokee claims in Texas

[3] Woldert, "The Last of the Cherokees in Texas," *loc. cit.*, 224n.
[4] *Tulsa Tribune*, Apr. 20, 1948.

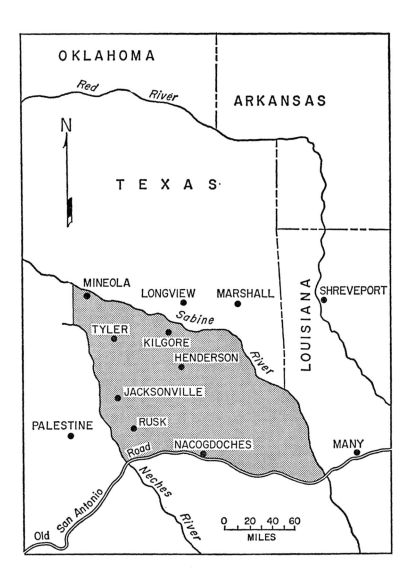

Shaded area shows land claimed by descendants of the Texas
Cherokees when their delegation appeared before the Indian
Claims Commission in 1948.

Courtesy *Tulsa Tribune* (April 20, 1948)

was filed in March, 1964, by Earl Boyd Pierce, of Muskogee, Oklahoma, general counsel of the Cherokee Nation. He proposed a method by which he believed that the Cherokees' claim could be settled "once and for all." Pierce stated that for many years the Cherokees had noted a lack of agreement among historians about the facts of the Cherokee question. His plan involved the appointment of a commission made up of three eminent historians, one of whom would be selected by the Cherokees, one by the state of Texas acting through the governor and attorney general, and the third by the first two appointees. The findings of the historians would be delivered to a legal panel of three prominent attorneys, similarly chosen, for recommendations which would be submitted by the governor and the attorney general to the Texas legislature.

In presenting his plan for final settlement, Pierce acknowledged that it would be impractical to cede or transfer title to the large domain claimed by the Texas Cherokees and stipulated that in no event was compensation in excess of one dollar an acre to be awarded. He further proposed that such cash settlement, if awarded, should be held in trust by the state of Texas for the benefit of the Cherokee Nation for a period of twenty-five years, the nation withdrawing only 5 per cent interest a year, an amount he estimated at approximately $100,000. This money would be used for the education of young Cherokees of one-half or more Indian blood. At the end of the twenty-five-year period, the trust thus created would be released and returned to the state of Texas, together with release of any and all claims, "moral or otherwise."

The Pierce proposal, submitted to Governor John Connally and Attorney General Waggoner Carr, was reviewed by Carr to determine the legality of such a settlement. In a rather long opinion issued on March 3, 1964, Carr quoted frequently from the record of treaties and correspondence involving the Cherokees. He held that any legal or moral claim which the Cherokees may have had would have been a claim against the Texas Republic, not the state of Texas, since the state of Texas did not come into existence until December, 1845. He quoted from the Constitution of Texas of 1845, which forbade appropriation of any money for the settlement of a claim, "real or pretended, where the same shall not have been provided for by pre-existing law." (However, that same section went on to say that nothing therein should be construed to affect claims against the Republic of Texas theretofore existing.)

Carr also cited the Texas Constitution of 1861, wherein much the same wording was used, and then the Constitution of 1876, which noticeably omitted mention of claims against the Republic of Texas. He ruled that such omission was evidence that the people of Texas did not intend to honor claims against the republic that had not been established by 1876.

Concluding his opinion, Carr stated positively that, if the Pierce plan was held valid by the proposed commissions, the settlement would require an appropriation of moneys by the legislature for which no authority existed under the Texas constitution. Therefore neither the governor nor the attorney general was legally authorized to enter into such a settlement.[5]

The Cherokees are persistent and patient. For the past century and more they and their descendants have maintained an organization to carry on litigation seeking compensation in the nation's courts. So far, none of the claims have resulted in success, but the Indians have not yet given up. Someday they may yet be reimbursed for the vast Neches–Sabine River lands which they once held in the "Red Lands" of East Texas, seized by the white man in his westward march to empire.

[5] Memorandum to Governor John Connally Concerning Cherokee Indian Claim Relating to Lands in Texas, *loc. cit.*

Epilogue

O<small>NE</small> day in the spring of 1968, my husband and I drove to Tyler, Texas, to see the azaleas and dogwood in bloom. After following the Azalea Trail in the city, we headed west out the old Dallas Highway. We drove about a dozen miles, crossed the Neches River, and turned off on a winding farm-to-market road. We admired the native trees, the pines, red oaks, sweetgums, and occasional blooming dogwood. To be sure we were on the right road, we stopped at a farmhouse and asked directions from a friendly farmer.

"We are hunting for the Cherokee battleground where Chief Bowles was killed," we told him.

"You're on the right track," he replied, and gave explicit directions, which led us to a farm home down the road, through a gate, and down a seldom-traveled private road. We soon came to a little plain above the Neches. Standing like a lonely sentinel in this natural clearing was the monument erected by the state of Texas in 1936, marking the spot where Chief Bowles had fallen.

All was still on that lovely spring day as we read the inscription:

On this site the Cherokee Chief Bowles was killed on July 16, 1839 while leading 800 Indians of various tribes in battle against 500

Texans. The last engagement between Cherokees and whites in Texas.

Suddenly, a redbird trilled its song from a near-by tree. Curious cattle wandered toward us as we stood there quietly. It was hard to believe that this peaceful spot had been a bloody battlefield on a hot July day well over a century before. We could envision old Chief Bowles astride his handsome sorrel, almost alone upon the field as his warriors fled. Like Horatius at the bridge, that gallant Cherokee warrior might well have said: "And how can man die better,/Than facing fearful odds/For the ashes of his fathers/And the temples of his gods." But Horatius was more fortunate.[1] He held his bridge. Chief Bowles died on that field of battle, and his people lost their Texas paradise.

[1] Ed Syers, *Off the Beaten Trail*, II, 74–77.

Bibliography

1. MANUSCRIPT MATERIALS

Asbury, Samuel E. Papers. East Texas Room, Paul L. Boynton Library, Stephen F. Austin State University, Nacogdoches. [Asbury taught history for many years at Texas A. & M. University and spent sixty years of his life collecting Texas history. Several filed newspaper articles pertain to the Texas Cherokees.]

Bexar Archives. Archives Collection, University of Texas Library, Austin. Translation. Commander of Texas to Austin, May 18, 1826, Blotter for 1825; Political chief to the Governor, October 2, 1825, Blotter for 1826; Political chief to Richard Fields, May 3, 1826; Austin to Ahumada, May 18, 1826.

Blake, R. B. Collection. Private library of Jenkins Garrett, Fort Worth. [One of seven sets in existence. Over thirty thousand pages in seventy-five volumes. These papers contain voluminous collections of official and private documents and proceedings relating to East Texas from the Mexican settlement of Nacogdoches and of San Antonio, or Bexar. Blake devoted over thirty years of his life to their compilation. Priceless to the student of early Texas history.]

Burnet, David G. Papers. Archives, University of Texas; State Archives, Austin; and Rosenberg Library, Galveston. [Since Burnet served as Vice-President under President Lamar, he not only conferred with Chief Bowles but fought in the Battle of the Neches. The Cherokees were a thorn in his flesh because their domain was on the grant which he failed to colonize.]

Carselowey, James M. "Cherokee Pioneers." P.O. Box 156, Adair, Okla., 1961.

———. "Early Settlers." P.O. Box 156, Adair, Okla., 1962.

———. "My Journal." P.O. Box 156, Adair, Okla., 1962.

Crocket, George. Papers. East Texas Room, Paul L. Boynton Library, Stephen F. Austin State University, Nacogdoches. [Crocket spent many years of his life collecting history of East Texas. He was planning a book on the East Texas Indians, and his preliminary materials are found throughout his papers. He and author Albert Woldert of Tyler (q.v.) carried on a brisk correspondence on the Cherokees. This correspondence is included in the Crocket papers.]

Fields, George W. Papers. Thomas Gilcrease Institute of American History and Art, Tulsa. [Among these papers is a typed article headed "Texas Cherokees, 1820–1839."]

Foreman, Grant. Papers. Indian Archives Division, Oklahoma Historical Society, Oklahoma City; Gilcrease Institute of American History and Art, Tulsa. [A valuable typed paper in this collection is entitled "The Bowle" and was copied from *American State Papers*.]

Indian and Pioneer Papers. "Interview with W. W. Harnage," by L. W. Wilson, March 19, 1937. Phillips Collection, University of Oklahoma, Norman.

Jackson, Andrew. Papers. The Library of Congress. Microfilms. North Texas State University, Denton. Series 1, Sept. 15, 1835, to April 4, 1837, Reel 47; Series 1, Nov. 15, 1816, to June 19, 1817, Reel 22; Series 1, June 20, 1817, to Jan. 18, 1818, Reel 23. [Quite a few Cherokee references are cited in these papers, but they do not pertain to the Texas Cherokees.]

Nacogdoches Archives. File 221. Typescript. Archives Collection, University of Texas Library, Austin.

Nacogdoches Archives. Files 197 and 209. Richard Fields to Samuel Norris, August 26, and to Austin, August 27, 1826. Typescript. Archives Collection, University of Texas Library, Austin.

Posey, James B. "A History of Cherokee Country." B. A. Thesis, University of Texas, 1928.

Record of Translations of Empresario Contracts, 85. Texas General Land Office, Austin.

Richey, Carrye Everett. "Thomas Jefferson Rusk and His Indian Campaigns." East Texas Room, Paul L. Boynton Library, Stephen

F. Austin State University, Nacogdoches. [This paper records Rusk's many skirmishes and battles with the Indians, and especially his part in the Cherokee War.]

Robertson, Sterling C. Papers. Malcolm McLean, Texas Christian University, Fort Worth, Texas.

Rusk, Thomas Jefferson. Papers. Archives, University of Texas, Austin; East Texas Room, Paul L. Boynton Library, Stephen F. Austin State University, Nacogdoches. [The voluminous Rusk Papers are important to the student of Indian history in East Texas, especially that of the Cherokee tribe. Rusk served as head of the Texas Militia during some of the major campaigns. He usually wrote a bold and legible hand, but some of his Indian reports are difficult to read. No doubt most of them were penciled in a tent after a grueling day on the frontier. Mrs. Lois Foster Blount, author of "A Brief Study of Thomas J. Rusk" (*q.v.*), worked for many years in the Paul L. Boynton Library, Nacogdoches. During her employment she found time to copy most of Rusk's letters and reports. Now, thanks to her, they are on file in the Rusk Papers of that university, convenient and easy to study.]

Sloan, Sallie Everett. "The Presidential Administration of David G. Burnet, March 17, October 22, 1836, With a Sketch of His Career." B. A. Thesis, University of Texas, 1918.

Sterrett, Carrie Belle. "The Life of Thomas Jefferson Rusk." M.A. Thesis, University of Texas, August, 1922.

Wahrhaftig, Albert L. "Social and Economic Characteristics of the Cherokee Population of Eastern Oklahoma." Report of a survey of six settlements in the Cherokee Nation. Carnegie Cross-Cultural Education Project of the University of Chicago, December, 1965.

2. GOVERNMENT DOCUMENTS

American State Papers. Indian Affairs, Vols. I and II. Washington, Gales and Seaton, 1834.

"Cherokee Agency East, 1824–1836." Letters received by the Office of Indian Affairs, 1824–80. General Services Administration. National Archives and Records Service. (Microfilms, University of Oklahoma.) [These letters contain much history of the Georgia

Cherokees before they immigrated to Indian Territory, but they do not mention the Texas Cherokees.]

"Cherokees West." Letters received by the office of Indian Affairs, 1824–36. General Services Administration. National Archives and Records Service. (Microfilms, University of Oklahoma.) [These papers deal mostly with Cherokee immigration to Arkansas. Chief Bowles is not mentioned.]

Congressional Record. 11 Cong., 2 sess., March 14, 1810. [William Scott, Pettigrew, *et al.*, seeking damages for Cherokee depredations.]

Hodge, Frederick Webb (ed.). *Handbook of American Indians North of Mexico.* Bureau of American Ethnology *Bulletin No. 30*, 2 Pts. Washington, 1907, 1910.

Journal of the Consultation Held at San Felipe de Austin, October 16, 1835. Barker Texas History Library, Austin.

Journal of the House of Representatives of the Republic of Texas, 1838, 1839. Texas State Library, Austin.

Memorandum to Governor John Connally Concerning Cherokee Indian Claim Relating to Lands in Texas. March 3, 1964. Attorney General's Office, Austin, Texas.

Mooney, James. *Myths of the Cherokee.* Bureau of American Ethnology *Report.* Pt. I. Washington, 1897–98.

Royce, Charles C. *The Cherokee Nation of Indians: A Narrative of Their Official Relations with the Colonial and Federal Governments.* Bureau of American Ethnology *Fifth Annual Report.* Pt. 2. Washington, 1887.

Secretary of War Letters, 1820–38, Military Affairs. National Archives. (Microfilms, Oklahoma Historical Society Library, Oklahoma City.)

Swanton, John R. *The Indian Tribes of North America.* Bureau of American Ethnology *Bulletin 145.* Washington, 1952.

Territorial Papers of the United States. Ed. by Clarence E. Carter. 27 vols. Washington, Government Printing Office, 1936.

3. Newspapers

Arkansas Gazette (Little Rock). May 26, 1821; May 29, 1827; Apr. 15, 1830; Mar. 14, 1832; July 19, 1836; Aug. 30, 1837; Sept. 19,

1837; July 3, 1839; and Aug. 28, 1839. [Many travelers to and from Texas passed through Arkansas in early days, and the editor of this lively weekly kept his columns filled with news of the Mexican Territory to the west, and later of the Republic of Texas. The student of Texas history should not overlook this valuable source of material. It may be seen on microfilms at Texas Christian University, Fort Worth.]

Cherokee Advocate (Tahlequah, Oklahoma). [This paper was founded in 1844. Its object was to encourage education and religion and to furnish information to its readers. The files are indexed at the Oklahoma State Historical Society, Oklahoma City, but there are no articles about the Texas Cherokees.]

Cherokee Phoenix (New Echota, Georgia). [This pioneer newspaper was founded by Elias Boudenot in 1824 and served as a mouthpiece for the many grievances of the Cherokees. There is no mention of Texas Cherokees.]

Courier-Times-Telegraph (Tyler, Texas). April 28, 1925; June 11, 1925.

Dallas Morning News. January 10, 1937; February 25, 1940; July 19, 1969.

Galveston Daily News. June 26, 1921.

Houston Telegraph. June 19, 1839.

Leeds Intelligencer (Leeds, England). March 8, 1791.

New Orleans Bee. July 29, 1839.

Niles' Weekly Register, 1814–37, and *Niles' National Register*, 1837–49 (Boston-Baltimore). [These papers are a source of valuable information about almost any phase of early American history. The editors carried articles of interest from all sections of the country, usually picked up from other publications; the Cherokees were often mentioned.]

Northern Standard (Clarksville, Texas). August 20, 1842, through March 26, 1853. [This newspaper contains much early history of Texas, including several stories about the Texas Cherokees. It may be seen on microfilms at the Carter Museum of Western Art, Fort Worth.]

Redlander (San Augustine). July 20, 1839.

Telegraph and Texas Register (San Felipe, Harrisburg, Columbia, and Houston). 1835–46. [This paper was known as "The Mouth Piece of the Texas Republic," and its pages contain early history that has not been recorded elsewhere.]

Texas Sentinel (Austin). June 15, 1840.

Tulsa Tribune. April 20, 1948.

4. BOOKS

Austin, Stephen F. *The Austin Papers*. Ed. by Eugene C. Barker. Austin, University of Texas Press, 1927.

Ballenger, T. L. *Around Tahlequah Council Fires*. Oklahoma City, Cherokee Publishing Company, Inc., 1945.

Bancroft, Hubert Howe. *History of the North Mexican States and Texas*. 23 vols. San Francisco, The History Company, 1890.

Barker, Eugene C. *Life of Stephen F. Austin, Founder of Texas, 1793–1836: A Chapter in the Westward Movement of the Anglo-American People*. Nashville, Cokesbury Press, 1926.

Barry, Ada Loomis. *Yunini's Story of the Trail of Tears*. London, Fudge and Company, The Mitre Press, 1932.

Bassett, John Spencer. *The Life of Andrew Jackson*. New York, The MacMillan Co., 1916.

Binkley, William C. *The Texas Revolution*. Baton Rouge, Louisiana State University Press, 1952.

Biographical Directory of the Texas Conventions and Congresses. Austin, Book Exchange, Inc., 1941.

Brown, John Henry. *History of Texas from 1685 to 1892*. 2 vols. St. Louis, L. E. Danielle, 1897.

———. *Indian Wars and Pioneers of Texas*. St. Louis, L. E. Danielle, 1897.

Brown, John P. *Old Frontiers: The Story of the Cherokee Indians from Earliest Times to the Dates of Their Removal to the West, 1838*. Kingsport, Southern Publication, Inc., 1938.

Clarke, Mary Whatley. *David G. Burnet, First President of Texas*. Austin, The Pemberton Press, 1969.

Cotterill, R. S. *The Southern Indians: The Story of the Civilized Tribes Before Removal*. Norman, University of Oklahoma Press, 1954.

Crocket, George L. *Two Centuries in East Texas: A History of San Augustine County and Surrounding Territory, from 1685 to the*

Present Time. Dallas, The Southwest Press, 1962. Facsimile Reproduction for the Christ Church, San Augustine.

Dale, Edward Everett, and Gaston Litton. *Cherokee Cavaliers.* Norman, University of Oklahoma Press, 1939.

Dale, Edward Everett. *The Indians of the Southwest.* Norman, University of Oklahoma Press, 1949.

Davidson, Donald. *The Tennessee.* Vol. II, *The New River: Civil War to TVA.* New York, Rinehart and Co., 1948.

Davis, M. E. M. *Under Six Flags: The Story of Texas.* Dallas, Cokesbury Book Store, 1897. The Teddlie Bindery, Midlothian, Texas. Facsimile edition.

DeShields, James T. *Border Wars of Texas, Being an Authentic and Popular Account, in Chronological Order, of the Long and Bitter Conflict Waged Between Savage Indian Tribes and the Pioneer Settlers of Texas.* Ed. by Matt Bradley. Tioga, Texas, The Herald Co., 1912.

Dorsey, George A. *Indians of the Southwest.* Passenger Department, Atchison, Topeka and Santa Fe Railroad System, 1903.

Douglas, C. L. *Cattle Kings of Texas.* Fort Worth, Branch-Smith, Inc., 1968.

Drake, Samuel S. *Biography and History of the Indians in North America.* Boston, Antiquarian Institute, 1837. Book I.

Duval, J. C. *Early Times in Texas.* Austin, H. P. N. Gammel and Co., 1892.

Eaton, Rachel Caroline. *John Ross and the Cherokee Indians.* Menasha, Wis., George Banta Publishing Co., 1914.

Foote, Henry Stuart. *Texas and the Texans.* 2 vols. Austin, Steck Company, 1935. [Facsimile reproduction.] Originally published in 1841.

Foreman, Carolyn Thomas. *Indians Abroad.* Norman, University of Oklahoma Press, 1936.

Foreman, Grant. *The Five Civilized Tribes.* Norman, University of Oklahoma Press, 1934.

———. *Indian Removal.* Norman, University of Oklahoma Press, 1953.

———. *Sequoyah.* Norman, University of Oklahoma Press, 1938.

Forman, S. E. *The Life and Writings of Thomas Jefferson.* Indianapolis, The Brown Merrill Co., 1900.

Frost, John. *The History of Mexico and Its Wars*. New Orleans, Armand Hawkins, 1882.

Gambrell, Herbert Pickens. *Mirabeau Buonaparte Lamar, Troubadour and Crusader*. Dallas, Southwest Press, 1934.

Gammel, H. P. N. *The Laws of Texas, 1822–1897*. 10 vols. Austin, The Gammel Book Co., 1898.

Gibson, A. M. *The Kickapoos: Lords of the Middle Border*. Norman, University of Oklahoma Press, 1963.

Govan and Livingood. *The Chattanooga Country, 1540–1951*. New York, E. P. Dutton and Co., Inc., 1952.

Graham, Philip. *Life and Poems of Mirabeau Lamar*. Chapel Hill, The University of North Carolina Press, 1938.

Green, Mary Rowena Maverick (ed.). *Samuel Maverick, Texan: 1803–1870*. New York, H. Wolff, 1952.

Gregory, Jack, and Rennard Strickland. *Sam Houston with the Cherokees, 1829–1833*. Austin, University of Texas Press, 1967.

Haywood, John. *The Natural and Aboriginal History of Tennessee up to the First Settlement Therein by the White People in the Year 1768*. Nashville, 1823.

History of Tennessee, with Sketches of Gibson, Obion, Weakley, Dyer, and Lake Counties. Nashville, The Goodspeed Publishing Company, 1887.

Horgan, Paul. *Great River*. New York, Holt, Rinehart and Winston, 1965.

Houston, Sam. *The Autobiography of Sam Houston*. Ed. by Donald Day and Harry Herbert Ullom. Norman, University of Oklahoma Press, 1954.

———. *The Writings of Sam Houston*. Ed. by Amelia W. Williams and Eugene C. Barker. 8 vols. Austin, University of Texas Press, 1938–43. [These papers contain many letters from Houston to Bowles and vice versa, as well as other papers pertaining to the Texas Cherokees. Houston condemned the Lamar administration for expelling the Cherokees from Texas.]

Hunter, John Dunn. *Manners and Customs of Several Indian Tribes Located West of the Mississippi*. Minneapolis, Ross and Haines, Inc., 1957. [Facsimile reproduction of original.]

Jackson, Helen Maria (Fiske) Hunt. *A Century of Dishonor*. Boston, Roberts Brothers, 1892.

James, Marquis. *Andrew Jackson, The Border Captain.* New York, Grosset and Dunlop, 1938.

———. *The Raven: A Biography of Sam Houston.* New York, Blue Ribbon Books, 1929.

Jefferson, Thomas. *The Papers of Thomas Jefferson.* 17 vols. Princeton, Princeton University Press, 1950.

Johnson, Frank W. *A History of Texas and Texans.* Ed. by Eugene C. Barker. Chicago, The American Historical Society, 1914.

Kennedy, William. *Texas: The Rise, Progress, and Prospects of the Republic of Texas.* London, K. Hastings, 1841.

Lamar, Mirabeau Buonaparte. *The Papers of Mirabeau Buonaparte Lamar.* Ed. by Charles A. Gulick, Jr., *et al.* 6 vols. Austin, Von Boeckmann-Jones, 1921–27. [Since Lamar was president during the expulsion of the Cherokees from Texas, his papers are invaluable. They carry much information about this tragic chapter of Texas history.]

Lay, Bennett. *The Lives of Ellis P. Bean.* Austin, The University of Texas Press, 1960.

Malone, Henry Thompson. *Cherokees of the Old South.* Athens, The University of Georgia Press, 1956.

Marshall, Thomas Maitland. *A History of the Western Boundary of the Louisiana Purchase, 1819–41.* Berkeley, University of California Press, 1914. Vol. II. California University Publications in History. 79 vols.

Moore, Jack. *The Killough Massacre.* Jacksonville, Texas, Kiely Printing Co., 1966.

Morton, Ohland. *Teran and Texas.* Austin, The Texas State Historical Association, 1948.

Myres, Sandra L. *The Autobiography of K. M. Van Zandt.* Fort Worth, Texas Christian University Press, 1969.

Nance, Joseph M. *After San Jacinto; The Texas Mexican Frontier, 1837–1841.* Austin, University of Texas Press, 1963.

Newcomb, W. W., Jr. *The Indians of Texas.* Austin, University of Texas Press, 1961.

Newell, Rev. C. *History of the Revolution in Texas, Particularly of the War of 1835 and '36.* Austin, The Steck Co., 1935. [Facsimile of the original.]

Nuttall, Thomas. "Nuttall's Journal of Travels into the Arkansas

Territory, October 2, 1818–February 18, 1830," in *Early Western Travels*, ed. by Reuben Gold Thwaites. Cleveland, 1904–1907. Vol. XVIII.

Padover, Saul K. *The Complete Jefferson*. New York, Duell, Sloan and Pearce, Inc., 1943.

Parker, Thomas V. *The Cherokee Indians*. New York, The Grafton Press, 1907.

Peithmann, Irvin M. *Red Men of Fire*. Springfield, Charles C. Thomas, 1964.

Pennybacker, Anna J. Hardwicke. *New History of Texas for Schools*. Austin, Mrs. Percy V. Pennybacker, 1895.

Procter, Ben H. *Not Without Honor: The Life of John H. Reagan*. Austin, University of Texas Press, 1962.

Ramsey, J. G. M. *The Annals of Tennessee to the End of the Eighteenth Century*. Philadelphia, J. B. Lippincott and Co., 1860.

Reagan, John H. *Memoirs*. Ed. by Walter F. McCaleb. New York, The Neale Publishing Company, 1906.

Roach, Hattie Joplin. *A History of Cherokee County*. Dallas, Southwest Press, 1934.

Roland, Charles P. *Albert Sidney Johnston: Soldier of Three Republics*. Austin, University of Texas Press, 1964.

Smithers, Harriet (ed.). *Journals of the Fourth Congress of the Republic of Texas, 1839–1840*. 3 vols. Austin, Von Boeckmann-Jones, 1931.

Smithwick, Noah. *The Evolution of a State; or, Recollections of Old Texas Days*. Compiled by Nanna Smithwick. Austin, Gammel Book Company, 1900.

Starkey, Marion L. *The Cherokee Nation*. New York, Alfred A. Knopf, 1946.

Starr, Emmett. *Cherokees West, 1794–1839*. Claremore, Okla., n.p., 1910.

―――. *History of the Cherokee Indians, Their Legends and Folklore*. Oklahoma City, The Warden Company, 1921.

―――. *Old Cherokee Families*. Norman, University of Oklahoma Foundation, 1968.

Streeter, Thomas W. *Bibliography of Texas, 1795–1845. Texas Imprints*. Cambridge, Harvard University Press, 1955. Vol. II, 1839, 1843. Also Part II, *Mexican Imprints, Relating to Texas, 1803–1845*.

Syers, Ed. *Off the Beaten Trail*. 2 vols. Fort Worth, F. L. Motheral Company, 1964.

Texas Almanac, 1961–1962. Dallas, The Dallas Morning News, 1962.

Texas Almanac and Emigrant's Guide for 1858. Galveston, Williard Richardson, *Galveston News*, 1858.

Thrall, Homer S. *A History of Texas from Earliest Settlements to the Year 1876*. New York, University Publishing Co., 1876.

———. *A Pictorial History of Texas from the Earliest Visits of European Adventurers to A.D. 1879*. St. Louis, N. D. Thompson and Co., 1879.

Tolbert, Frank X. *The Day of San Jacinto*. New York, McGraw-Hill Book Co., Inc., 1959.

Washburn, Cephas. *Reminiscences of the Indians*. Ed. by Hugh Park. Van Buren, Argus Press, 1955.

Webb, Walter Prescott, *et al.* (eds.). *The Handbook of Texas*. 2 vols. Austin, Texas State Historical Association, 1952.

Webb, Walter Prescott. *The Texas Rangers: A Century of Frontier Defense*. New York, Houghton Mifflin Company, 1935.

Wharton, Clarence R. *The Republic of Texas: A Brief History of Texas, from the First American Colonies in 1821 to Annexation in 1846*. Houston, C. C. Young Printing Co., 1922.

———. *Texas Under Many Flags*. 5 vols. Chicago, American History Society, Inc., 1930.

Wilbarger, J. W. *Indian Depredations in Texas*. Austin, The Steck Company, 1935. [Facsimile of original.]

Williams, Alfred Mason. *Sam Houston and the War of Independence in Texas*. Boston, Houghton Mifflin Co., 1893.

Williams, Samuel Cole. *Adair's History of the American Indians*. Edited under the auspices of the National Society of the Colonial Dames of America in Tennessee. Johnson City, The Watauga Press, 1930.

———. *Tennessee During the Revolutionary War*. Nashville, The Tennessee Historical Commission, 1944.

Winfrey, Dorman H. "The Battle of the Neches," in *Battles of Texas*. Waco, Texian Press, 1967.

Winfrey, Dorman H., *et al.* (eds.). *Texas Indian Papers, 1825–1916*. 4 vols. Austin, Texas State Library, 1959, 1960.

Winkler, Ernest William (ed.). *Secret Journals of the Senate, Republic of Texas, 1836–1845.* Austin, Austin Printing Co., 1911.

Wisehart, M. K. *Sam Houston, American Giant.* Washington, Robert B. Luce, Inc., 1962.

Woodward, Grace Steele. *The Cherokees.* Norman, University of Oklahoma Press, 1963.

Wooten, Dudley G. (ed.). *A Comprehensive History of Texas, 1685 to 1899.* 2 vols. Dallas, William G. Scarff, 1898.

Wortham, Louis J. *A History of Texas, from Wilderness to Commonwealth.* 5 vols. Fort Worth, Wortham-Molyneaux Co., 1924.

Yoakum, Henderson. *History of Texas, from Its First Settlement in 1685 to Its Annexation to the United States in 1846.* 2 vols. New York, J. S. Redfield, 1855.

5. ARTICLES

Abel, Annie Heloise. "History of Events Resulting in Indian Consolidation West of the Mississippi," *American Historical Association Annual Report,* Vol. I (1906).

Almonte, Juan N. "Statistical Report on Texas," translated by Carlos E. Castaneda, *Southwestern Historical Quarterly,* Vol. XXVIII, No. 3 (July, 1924–Apr., 1925).

Bandy, Mrs. B. J. "Old Van House," *Chronicles of Oklahoma,* Vol. XXXII, No. 1 (1954).

Blount, Lois Foster. "A Brief Study of Thomas J. Rusk, Based on His Letters to His Brother David, 1835–1856," *Southwestern Historical Quarterly,* Vol. XXXIV, Nos. 3 and 4 (July, 1930–Apr., 1931).

Burton, Morris S. "The Cherokee War, 1839," *Chronicles of Smith County* (Texas), Vol. V, No. 2 (Fall, 1966).

Christian, A. K. "Mirabeau Buonaparte Lamar," *Southwestern Historical Quarterly,* Vol. XXIII, No. 3 (July, 1919–Apr., 1920), and Vol. XXIV, Nos. 1, 2, 3, 4 (July, 1920–Apr., 1921).

Clark, Blake. "America's Greatest Earthquake," condensed from *Shreveport Magazine. Reader's Digest* (Apr., 1969).

Daniell, Forrest. "Texas Pioneer Surveyors and Indians," *Southwestern Historical Quarterly,* Vol. LX, No. 4 (July, 1956–Apr., 1957).

Fait, Anna R. "An Autobiography by Anna R. Fait," *Chronicles of Oklahoma*, Vol. XXXII, No. 2 (1954–55).

Fields, Dorothy Louise. "David Gouverneur Burnet," *Southwestern Historical Quarterly*, Vol. XLIX, No. 2 (1945–46).

Foreman, Carolyn T. "An Early Account of the Cherokees," *Chronicles of Oklahoma*, Vol. XXXIV, No. 2 (1946).

Foreman, Grant. "Dwight Mission," *Chronicles of Oklahoma*, Vol. XII (Mar.–Dec., 1934).

———. "The Story of Sequoyah's Last Days," *Chronicles of Oklahoma*, Vol. XII (Mar.–Dec., 1934).

Gray, Frederick T. "Indians of North America," *The North American Review*, Vol. XXII, No. 1 (1826).

Johnson, Judge N. B. "A Historical Relic at Tahlequah," *Chronicles of Oklahoma*, Vol. XLIV, No. 2 (Summer, 1966).

King, V. O. "The Cherokee Nation of Indians," *Quarterly of the Texas State Historical Association*, Vol. II, No. 1 (July, 1898).

Knight, Oliver. "History of the Cherokees," *Chronicles of Oklahoma*, Vol. XXXIV, No. 2 (1956).

Koch, Lena Clara. "The Federal Indian Policy in Texas, 1845–1860," *Southwestern Historical Quarterly*, Vol. XXVIII, No. 4 (July, 1924–Apr., 1925).

Loye, Dave. "Cherokee Country," *Oklahoma Today*, Vol. IX, No. 4 (Fall, 1960).

McClendon, R. Earl. "The First Treaty of the Republic of Texas," *Southwestern Historical Quarterly*, Vol. LII, No. 2 (1948–49).

Muckleroy, Anna. "The Indian Policy of the Republic of Texas," *Southwestern Historical Quarterly*, Vol. XXV, No. 4 (1922); Vol. XXVI, No. 1 (1923).

Reagan, John H. "Expulsion of the Cherokees from East Texas," *Quarterly of the Texas State Historical Association*, Vol. I (1897–98).

Sanchez, José María. "A Trip to Texas in 1828," tr. by Carlos E. Castaneda, *Southwestern Historical Quarterly*, Vol. XXIX, No. 4 (1926).

Spillman, W. J. "Adjustment of the Texas Boundary in 1850," *Quarterly of the Texas State Historical Association*, Vol. VII, No. 3 (July, 1903–Apr., 1904).

Stanley, Mildred. "Cherokee Indians in Smith County," *Texas History Teachers Bulletin*, Vol. XII, No. 1 (Oct., 1924).

Stayton, Robert W. "Thomas J. Rusk," *Texas Law Review*, Vol. XLIV (October, 1925).

Winfrey, Dorman H. "Chief Bowles of the Texas Cherokee," *Chronicles of Oklahoma*, Vol. XXXII, No. 1 (1954).

Winkler, Ernest William. "The Cherokee Indians in Texas," *Quarterly of the Texas State Historical Association*, Vol. VII, No. 1 (July, 1903–Apr., 1904).

Woldert, Albert. "The Last of the Cherokees in Texas, and the Life and Death of Chief Bowles," *Chronicles of Oklahoma*, Vol. I, No. 2 (1921–23).

6. Miscellaneous

Interview with T. L. Ballenger, Tahlequah. [Retired history professor in Northeastern Oklahoma State College, an authority on Indian history and research. Author of *Around Tahlequah Council Fires*. Professor Ballenger recently sold his collection of papers to Newberry Library, Chicago.]

Interview with J. J. Hill, librarian, Bizzell Memorial Library, University of Oklahoma, Norman. [Mr. Hill compiled the comprehensive index for *Old Cherokee Families*, reprinted from *History of the Cherokee Indians, Their Legends and Folklore*, by Emmet Starr.]

Index